Hogarth. Self-portrait. Victoria & Albert Museum, London

The Meaning and Wonder of

art

by Fred Gettings

Golden Press • New York

Stradanus. Artist in his studio with apprentices. British Museum

contents

© 1963 Golden Pleasure Books, Ltd.
Printed in the U.S.A.

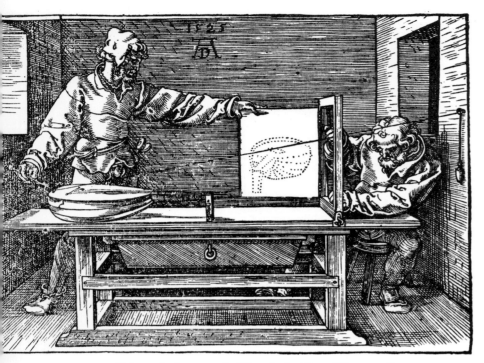

Dürer. Artist at work. Victoria & Albert Museum, London

Rembrandt. Self-portrait. National Gallery, London

English ivory Christ, 14th century.
Victoria & Albert Museum, London

8

Bewick. The hare. Author's collection

foreword

In a sense this book is about magic, for an artist is a kind of magician. He tries to do what is quite impossible—to take lifeless matter, such as paint, stone or clay, and mould it into a living form. The painter's brush is rather like a magic wand with which he can give life to something that appears to be dead.

Some five hundred years ago an English sculptor carved a lovely figure of Christ out of hard and lifeless ivory. With only a few coloured paints the Dutch artist Rembrandt created a portrait of himself which seems on the very point of moving into life. Thomas Bewick, the English artist, engraved a piece of solid wood to print a picture of a hare that is incredibly full of movement and vitality. All this is magic.

Art, as you will find in the following pages, is a very wonderful thing, and the study of art is a wonderful adventure. Such an adventure leads into an exciting world, so immense and so varied that no one can fully explore it. Once discovered and entered, however, this world can never be forgotten, for the treasures it has to offer—its meaning and its beauty—can make our life richer and more exciting.

This book is designed for those who wish to start on this adventure, to enter into this marvellous world of art. It deals with the practical side of art, with the basic laws of painting and sculpture, explaining the reasons why an artist creates in the way he does. Something of the astounding world in which he lives is revealed; a world where a seashell can inspire the design for a Greek column or a bishop's staff, and where a curved line can stand for a kangaroo! The book also deals as simply as possible with the more theoretical side of art, with such things as the mathematics behind a cathedral and the laws of composition in painting. How modern Science has affected painting and sculpture is explained and illustrated, while the mysteries and beauties of abstract painting are also discussed.

In effect the book will reveal the magic of art to those who feel that it has something to offer, and are not sure how to make the approach. The exciting ideas on each page will appeal alike to the bright child and inquiring adult, helping towards a deeper understanding of the meaning and beauty of art. Above all, the refreshing presentation of the book will encourage the reader to look at pictures and sculpture in an entirely new way; in a way which will allow a true and personal love for art to grow.

Breughel. Artist with connoisseur. Albertina, Vienna

9

Copy from mediaeval psalter. Two men leading Christ to Herod

Van Eyck. Head of Christ the King.
Church of St Bavon, Ghent

Holbein. Miniature of Mrs Pemberton.
Victoria & Albert Museum, London

Genesis Initial. Dean and Chapter, Winchester Cathedral

10

the reason why

An artist paints for many reasons. He may want to tell a story, like the Mediaeval monk who painted a picture of Christ being dragged to King Herod; or he may simply want to decorate a page of writing with a beautiful letter. On the other hand he may be asked to paint someone's portrait as a record for a relative or a friend. Holbein's beautiful little picture of a lady from the Court of Henry VIII is a fine example of this.

Perhaps a wish to capture a brief effect of light made Monet paint the Houses of Parliament seen in the fog. It was probably Van Eyck's aim to express the might and power of God in his picture of Christ in majesty. Sometimes artists spend much of their time and skill in making beautiful things which will serve a useful purpose. The man seated on the lion is really a candle-stick—not all candlesticks are designed and made with such loving care!

As we can see, an artist needs to create for many different reasons. His purpose in life, it seems, is to make Beauty for men to enjoy.

And in a special sense we are all artists, for a need to make Beauty exists in all of us. We like to dress nicely, for instance, or to arrange our rooms so that they are tidy and pleasant to live in. Maybe you enjoy arranging flowers in a bowl, or knitting and sewing beautiful things. Perhaps you like working in the garden, putting much effort into making it look nice. Or you may go in for drawing and painting in your spare time as a hobby. Most of us spend time, effort and care in making something beautiful, just as an artist does. Such activities spring from the need to create which lies in us all.

When you 'decorate' your school books with little drawings in the margin, you are doing so for the same reasons as the artists who decorated the hand-written Bibles before the invention of printing. The urge is the same, but your skill is quite probably less than that of the real artist.

Besides the difference in ability, there is another difference between ourselves and artists: the artist usually feels much more strongly than we do this urge to make beautiful things. Sometimes it is as if he is driven in spite of himself to express a sort of beauty which is hidden from ordinary eyes, and we find it difficult to understand what he means. He is rather like someone trying to describe to a blind man what the world looks like—a thing so difficult to do that only some very strong force can keep an artist trying.

Flemish bronze candlestick (Samson and the lion), 13th century. Victoria & Albert Museum, London

Monet. Houses of Parliament in the fog. Louvre, Paris

Bewick. Chillingham bull. Victoria & Albert Museum, London

Minoan vase with bull decoration. British Museum

men, caves and bulls

Back in the dawn of civilisation when Man lived in caves, wearing nothing but skins and hunting for food like a wild animal, he was an artist. Because he wanted beautiful things around him he carved wood, bones and rocks into lively shapes. He scratched designs on the walls of his cave and coloured them with dyes and clays, and in spite of his crude tools he made pictures of an incredible vitality and beauty.

His first subjects were animals—perhaps because of their importance to him as food. Many primitive people believe that a picture of a thing is as real as the thing itself—that if they possess a picture of an animal, then they have some strange power over that animal. This is the reason why many primitive tribes in Africa still refuse to have their photographs taken, for they think that if the photographer has a picture of them they will become his slaves! An amusing but true story is told of an Indian of North America, who saw an artist drawing bison at the time when they were becoming scarce in America. The Indian believed that the bison

Egyptian wall-painting. Inspecting cattle. British Museum

Sumerian stone bull,
c. 3000 B.C. British Museum

Goya. Bull, c. late 18th century. British Museum

Bull from Lascaux Caves, prehistoric

were scarce *because* the artist was drawing them. As he said to a friend, "I know this man has put many of our bison into his book. I was there when he did it, and since then we have had no bison!"

Perhaps this is why prehistoric men painted animals on their cave walls, in the belief that if they owned their images, they owned the animals themselves. In a sense, why they painted animals isn't very important to our study of art. What is important, though, is that they *did* paint them.

Nothing can teach us more about art than a careful comparison between the different ways in which artists have painted similar things. From this page we can see how art has changed only very little in thousands of years. The way in which cavemen, some 22,000 years ago, saw and painted bulls is very much like the way the Spanish artist Goya saw and painted bulls only 150 years ago. In fact the most striking thing about these pictures is how similar the general *feel* of the bulls are, in spite of the different periods and different methods of painting.

Drawing after prehistoric cave painting 13

Pottery bull, Chinese 4th century A. D. British Museum

Ivory bull from Irak, c. 700 B.C.
City Museum and Art Gallery, Birmingham

more bulls

Of course, there *are* differences. The drawing of a bull which is taken from a wall painting in the island of Crete is very different from the painting of a bull from Picasso's picture "Guernica". The Cretan artist was very much concerned with the shape of the bull, and with the way he could suggest its movement. Picasso, on the other hand, although he is still interested in the shape of the bull, is more concerned with what the bull is, and how it acts. His painting expresses the savage cruelty of the bull.

One of the basic ways of beginning to understand about art is by asking questions about pictures. Look carefully at all these bulls, and try to find out why some of them are so alike, and why some of them are so different. Try to work out in your mind why the artist painted these bulls in the particular way he did; ask yourself for what reason he painted them. What was it about the bull which interested him so much that he wanted to paint it? Try to ask similar questions of yourself when you look at other pictures in this book or in art galleries.

Sumerian bull from East Turkey,
c. 2500 B.C. British Museum

14

Bull's head from Knossos. Herakleion Museum

Bull's head from East Turkey,
8th century B.C. British Museum

Bull dancers. Wall-painting from Knossos. Herakleion Museum

Picasso. Guernica 1937 (detail). Museum of Modern Art,
New York

Rembrandt. Head of girl.
Victoria & Albert Museum, London

German Baroque crucifix
figure, 17th century.
Victoria & Albert
Museum, London

Danish Romanesque crucifix
figure, c. 1150. Victoria &
Albert Museum, London

African mask, 19th century.
British Museum

style in art

All the pictures of bulls we saw on the last page were different in style.

Style is a personal thing: it comes from an individual reaction to a given task. We all write in different styles, for instance. Although there are millions of people in the world, no two people write in exactly the same way. Some people don't bother to cross their 't's, some write with a flourish, others scrawl, whilst others are very neat—but they all write differently. If you are throwing a ball, you do so in your own particular way. It doesn't matter how high or how far you throw it, you still throw it in the way which is special to yourself. Perhaps someone else could throw it higher than you—but they couldn't throw it in exactly the same way. This is your style.

It is exactly the same with an artist. If he sets out to paint something, he will paint it in his own special way. Certain things about the subject he is painting or drawing will catch his attention and interest him, and these will become important to his work. These things help to make his personal style. Picasso's interest in the savageness of the bull makes his painting different from that of the artist who was interested mainly in its pattern. The different interests result in different styles.

Take for instance these two pieces of carving. One is a Danish crucifix figure made in 1150 A.D., whilst the other is a crucifix figure made in Germany 500 years later. They are both of the same subject but they are in very different styles. It would be wrong to say that because the Danish figure is less realistic and more stiff than the other, it is not as good a work of art. They are both beautiful works of art in their own individual ways. The Danish crucifix figure is in the *Romanesque* style whereas the German is in the *Baroque* style.

The Danish artist was not interested in the same problems as the German artist—he didn't want to produce a statue that was realistic. He probably wanted his statue to look as stiff as possible so that it would blend into the severe church architecture of the day. By making it stiff and unnatural he has increased its religious meaning, suggesting that this is the figure of no ordinary man—but of one from Heaven. The large eyes and mouth somehow make the face more alive than a mere copy of a face would.

It is obvious that this stiffness was not the aim of the German artist. He wanted to make his figure look like an ordinary man in great pain. The two pieces of carving are different in style because the artist's aims and interests were different.

Let us look at two more different styles. When Paul Klee, the Swiss artist, drew this head of a girl he wanted to convey many things. He was experimenting in using simple lines to suggest colour, which in some uncanny way this drawing succeeds in doing. He also wanted to convey a sense of a new and fanciful world where such a girl could live. It is as if Klee suddenly grew tired of being an adult artist and wanted to draw in a childlike way. His drawing certainly has caught something of that fresh innocence which exists in drawings by very young children. Perhaps he was a little influenced by the tribal masks of African natives for the idea behind his drawing, for a great similarity between the two styles can be seen.

Rembrandt also drew the head of a young girl wearing a hat, but this time with very different aims in view. He wanted to create a head which could live in a world much like our own: in a world of light and shade. Maybe it was the way in which light fell across the girl's face which caught Rembrandt's interest, or perhaps he wanted to catch her look of sadness.

Both the Rembrandt and the Klee drawings express more than a photograph can. A photograph records only the light as it falls on the world from the sun or from an electric lamp. It records only appearance. But a great artist, like Rembrandt or Klee, can somehow go more deeply than the surface appearance, and record feelings and hidden things, like sadness and innocence. Both these drawings are of the same subject, and yet they are quite different in style.

Paul Klee. Copy of 'The hat does it'

Breughel. Children's games. Kunsthistorisches Museum, Vienna

building a picture

When you arrange a vase of flowers in the centre of the table to decorate a room, you are doing much the same as an artist who paints a picture. The colours of the flowers and the length of their stems are as important as the exact spot where you put the vase. You will arrange the flowers so that they look nice, cutting their stems if necessary, and perhaps rearranging one or two of the flowers. You will look at the vase from different angles, considering its position carefully, and only when you are quite satisfied with the arrangement will you leave it. When an artist paints a picture he does almost exactly the same thing. He arranges his colours, lines and shapes on the canvas or paper in the way which he thinks will best suit his purpose. The manner in which he arranges these three things is called his *composition*.

Just as a house is built brick by brick, so is a picture built line by line, colour by colour. If the bricks of the house are not well placed, the walls will fall down and the house will be useless. So, if the colours and lines are not properly arranged, the composition of the picture will be bad, and the artist will not succeed in conveying his meaning. The picture will be useless.

Here we have two examples of different compositions —one is very simple, the other is more complicated. The painting by Breughel, a Dutch artist, of children playing games, is full of detail and interest; the eye is drawn from one little incident to the next, for the colours, lines and shapes have been arranged in a very complex way. Nevertheless, the picture is organised— it isn't just a canvas teeming with detail, for it has an underlying order. Its composition, though so complicated, is pleasant to look at. Goya's little Spanish girl is painted in a very simple way. The eye is held by the one figure, and finds sufficient interest in this alone. As the figure is well placed and the arrangement is pleasant, the composition, though simple, is good.

Breughel painted his picture full of details and closely packed shapes to convey a sense of the bustling move-ment of children playing games. Goya, on the other hand, didn't want to create movement. Because his model came from a rich and proud Spanish family he wanted to suggest a sense of quiet dignity. Accordingly, he painted her portrait in a manner that would convey this dignity.

Thus, when we talk about composition we mean the way in which the lines, colours and shapes have been arranged to convey some particular meaning or effect.

How the artist goes about building his compositions· to convey some particular meaning is very interesting, and will form the subject of the next few pages.

Goya. Senora Sabasa Garcia. National Gallery of Art, Washington, D.C.

Breughel. Artist with connoisseur. Albertina, Vienna

19

triangles and pictures

If you've ever watched new office blocks or flats being built, you will know that the builders first of all erect a sort of framework out of steel girders around which the building is constructed. In this way, the building has a firm structure and will be quite safe. It is very similar in painting. The artist must build his composition on a firm structure which will serve to hold the picture together when it has been painted. Let us have a look at one of the ways a painter might construct this framework—starting off with a triangle.

In the first diagram (A), we have a triangle drawn within the frame of the picture. It is balancing on one of its points, and looks as if it might fall over at any minute. This would not be a very good scaffold to build a picture around.

But now, if we turn it over, as in diagram (B), we have a good firm triangle standing solidly on its base,

Pollaiuolo. Martyrdom of St Sebastian. National Gallery, London

20

Memlinc. Madonna and Child. National Gallery, London

like a pyramid. This won't fall over. Many painters have used this triangle as the basis for their composition: particularly in pictures of the Mother and Child. Memlinc's 'Virgin and Child' is a good example. In it you can see quite clearly the underlying composition of a triangle. The picture of the martyrdom of St Sebastian by Pollaiuolo, the Italian painter, is an example of a triangle composition holding together an intricate subject within its three straight lines.

Now let's try moving the top of the triangle a little over to the left. We still have a triangle firm on its base, but now with a much more interesting shape. The different lengths of the sides add a little variety, and form the sort of composition often used by portrait painters. Rembrandt's picture of a soldier is based on this structure.

Rembrandt. Portrait of a soldier. Glasgow Art Gallery

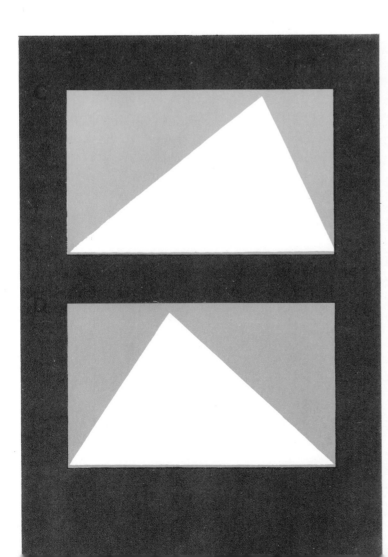

Georges de la Tour. Madonna and Child. Musée de Rennes

more triangles

Perhaps we can try two triangles as a basis for the composition. They are both firm on the ground, but the 'M' shape tends to be just a little boring. However, if we make the second triangle a bit smaller we get a very interesting composition. If we look carefully at the picture by Georges de la Tour, the seventeenth century French artist, we shall see that it is clearly based on a composition formed from two triangles.

Usually an artist only bases his composition on a particular geometrical form—he does not stick to the form completely, otherwise the picture would be boring because it lacked variety. For instance, in the painting by the Italian Giovanni Bellini, we can quite clearly see the three triangles which form the basis for its composition. We have the central triangle which is formed by the Madonna and Child, and we have also the two side triangles formed by St Catherine and Mary Magdalene. But within the framework of these three basic shapes Bellini has tried to create as much variety as possible. All the hands are placed differently; the faces are seen from different angles; and there is even a fourth triangle enclosing the Christ Child to the left of the picture. All this variety adds interest to the picture, yet does not at the same time destroy the underlying composition.

Sometimes an artist gets tired of a particular composition and sets out to paint a picture which seems to contradict all the rules. Van Eyck was a great Flemish painter, and very familiar with the use of triangular compositions to give a feeling of stability and rest, yet in his picture of a man in a turban, he seems to forget or ignore all he knows. The man's face and turban very clearly form a triangle—but this time it is upside-down! And yet, in spite of this, the composition of the picture feels perfect.

Great artists can do this—their mastery of their subject is such that they can disregard all the rules and still produce a great work of art. If we look a little more closely at this picture we shall be able to find out why it is a success, in spite of its contradiction of the rules.

In the first instance, the triangular shape of the head and turban is so very carefully placed in relation to the background that it feels perfect. Van Eyck has painted the turban with such loving accuracy of detail, and has arranged it so beautifully, that it catches and holds our attention. In this way our eyes are drawn to the top of the picture and are held there by the fascinating craftsmanship of the folds. Our interest and attention pins

Giovanni Bellini. Madonna with two saints. Academy, Venice

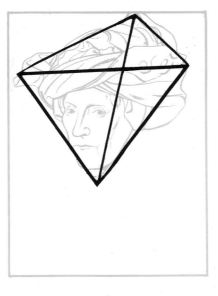

the triangle to the top of the picture area, and prevents it from giving the impression of sliding down.

Secondly, Van Eyck has taken into account our own imagination. Although we can't see the man's shoulders clearly, we do know they are there. When we look at the picture we don't think of there being simply a head without shoulders, hanging in empty space — we imagine the shoulders as well. In fact, our imagination creates quite a different composition from the one which is actually there. We imagine another triangle, balanced firmly on the base of the picture-frame, which supports the upside-down triangle.

So, whereas we thought Van Eyck was 'breaking the rules' he was, in fact, using them in an unexpected way.

Jan van Eyck. Portrait of a man in a red turban.
National Gallery, London

23

rest, dignity and movement

Just as an artist might use a triangle in his composition to give a feeling of stability, so he might use other lines and shapes to suggest other feelings. Take, for instance, these three diagrams. Each rectangle contains six lines drawn in different ways, and because of this they each have a different *feeling* about them. The first rectangle, with the horizontal lines, reminds us of a landscape and gives us a feeling of calm restfulness. The second has a feeling of dignity about it; possibly because it recalls the interior of a church or a forest of tall trees. The third is full of energy and movement, and is much more alive in feeling than the other two.

The artist often makes use of these three arrangements of line when building his compositions for a picture. If he wants a feeling of rest in his painting he will use the horizontal lines. If he wants a feeling of dignity he will use the vertical lines. And to create a feeling of energetic life he will use the curved lines of the third rectangle.

Let us look first at the way he would use the horizontal lines. When painting a landscape, an artist usually wants to convey a sense of the peace and quiet of the countryside, so he emphasises those lines which are horizontal. Constable's painting of Malvern Hall is a good example of the use of horizontals. Here, certainly, he has conveyed the quietness of the countryside. Notice how he has broken the horizontal lines formed by the tree-tops and their reflection in the river to lead our eye to the house, which is the subject of the picture. The other painting by Constable is even more obviously based on a series of horizontals which cut right across the rectangle of the frame. He breaks the monotony of the horizontals with the vertical trees and with the lovely texture of the leaves.

Sometimes an artist uses horizontal lines in connection with other geometrical shapes, such as the triangle. The portrait by Rembrandt in which the basic triangle shape is broken into sections by horizontals is a fine example. The horizontals add a feeling of quietness and calm to the stability of the triangle.

George Stubbs, one of the greatest animal painters, has composed this picture with a main triangle and four horizontals. See how cleverly he has varied the lines which form this basic framework, so that the geometry of the design shows through, yet is not too obvious.

Constable. Malvern Hall. National Gallery, London

Rembrandt. Portrait of a lady with an ostrich feather. National Gallery of Art, Washington, D.C.

24

Stubbs. Mares and foals with landscape. Ascot Collection, National Trust

Constable. Water-meadows near Salisbury.
Victoria & Albert Museum, London

Velasquez. Surrender of Breda. Prado, Madrid

spears and columns

Velasquez, the Spanish artist, painted this picture to commemorate the Spanish victory at Breda in 1625. We can see the defeated Dutch leader handing over the keys of the city to the Spanish general, who receives them with military dignity. His army is proud of its success, and the lances are held high in the air. The defeated Dutch, however, have nothing to be proud of, and all we can see held aloft are three flags and two halberds—which are far from proudly borne. Velasquez here makes very clever use of the feeling suggested by vertical and upright lines—a feeling of solemn dignity and pride.

Cathedrals and churches make much use of straight verticals in their columns, which soar high towards heaven. Nothing is more impressive than a Gothic or Romanesque aisle, with its rows of columns on either side, and its perpendicular stained-glass windows at the East End above the altar. Such a building is designed to impress the congregation with the dignity of the Church and God.

Very often, both verticals and horizontals together are used to give a composition a sense of dignity and rest. The best examples are Greek buildings such as the Parthenon, where the upward line is repeated by the many columns, and the horizontal is repeated at the top and bottom by the steps and roof decorations.

In painting, much the same is done. Here we have two examples, painted in Holland, one from the seventeenth century, and the other from modern times. The first is by Pieter de Hooch, and the other by Mondrian. There is a very striking resemblance between the construction of these pictures, but they were, of course, painted with very different aims in view. Pieter de Hooch wanted to reveal to the eye all the charms of a home in Holland, with its lovely light effects and delightful colours. He constructed his picture with an underlying composition of verticals and horizontals because he wanted to suggest the sleepy calm and quiet dignity of the house.

Mondrian, on the other hand, constructed a picture which would interest the eye with its interplay of crossing lines and small areas of colour. His picture is not of any particular subject, and his aim was to paint a surface which would entertain the eye in the same way as music entertains the ear.

Both artists use similar compositions for very different reasons, yet in both pictures the crossing verticals and horizontals pass on a feeling of dignity and rest.

Interior of Bourges Cathedral.
Photo Marburg

Mondrian. Painting in blue and yellow.
National Gallery of Art, Washington,
D.C.

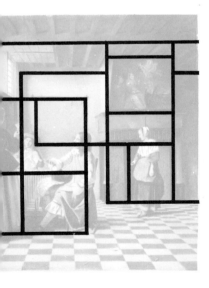

de Hooch. Interior with soldiers. National Gallery, London

Rubens. Bearing the Cross. Royal Museum of Fine Arts, Brussels

kangaroos and battles

Fifty or sixty years ago, a native of central Australia carved these curling lines on a piece of wood to decorate it. Just over two thousand years ago an artist drew a very similar pattern on a piece of stone—probably for the same reason. Neither of the patterns appear to represent anything (though the Australian native said that each of his curves was a 'kangaroo'!), but they do convey a strong sense of movement. Such spiral curves have often been used by artists for decorative purposes. When an artist paints a picture with a composition rich with such twists and curves, it is usually a picture full of action and movement. The Flemish artist Rubens has done this in his picture of Christ bearing the Cross— and how full of movement it is. The eye is caught, and zig-zags restlessly over the picture surface from point to point through the tangle of twisting forms. Movement for the sheer love of movement seems to be Rubens's aim in this instance.

The picture by Victor Pasmore, a modern English painter, has a composition based on swirling lines which is very pleasant to look at. The lines in his painting are much more organised—put into little sections, as it were. They have been carefully arranged into a sort of order, and because of this the eye does not tire easily. Paolo Uccello, the Italian painter, wanted to convey the movement of battle in his painting of knights fighting, but he realised the difficulties of com-

Pottery vase from Phaistos. Herakleion Museum

Bronze votive pin from Luristan (Persia). British Museum

Uccello. Battle of San Romano. National Gallery, London

Prehistoric grave carving

Pasmore. Inland seashore. Tate Gallery, London

posing such a scene. He knew that too much fiddling movement distracts the eye, and so he built his composition out of large swirling lines, which convey the movement without becoming too turbulent or fussy. Notice the large spiral which can be traced through the picture from the top right-hand corner, through the edge of the field, down the knight on the white horse, along the objects scattered on the ground, and up through the horses and knights on the right of the picture. Another curve runs down the white lance on the left, and under the knight's horse to link up with the other spiral. These two main curves link together all the figures in a good compositional whole. The painting is, in fact, full of such curves which intertwine and produce movement over the surface of the canvas.

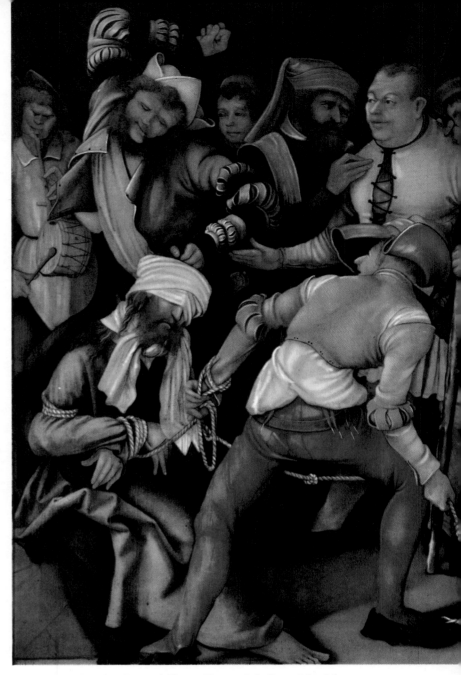

Grünewald. The mocking of Christ. National Gallery, Munich

rhythm in composition

Great painters use the rhythm in their compositions to convey a particular feeling. Let us take a look at two pictures with different rhythms, to find out how an artist might use rhythm to express something.

Grünewald, the German artist, used the rhythm of his painting to link together the three main figures in his composition. It is a strong, obvious rhythm which starts at the rope in the bottom right-hand corner of the picture and runs up the man's hand and arm, through his back, and down the left arm. It continues without a break along Christ's arm, up through His head, and then joins up with the left arm of the man who is standing behind Him. After running through his face and right arm, the rhythm ends abruptly in a clenched fist which is held back, ready to strike Christ a heavy and vicious blow. The rhythm is well constructed: it runs through most of the picture-area in a well-balanced way. But it is the way it runs which is of most interest. It is full of rapid movement, rather like a writhing snake, pulling the eye first in one direction and then in another. In itself it conveys the idea of agonised movement, and is very suited to the subject of the picture.

That Christ is being beaten is left in no doubt whatsoever—the rhythm starts off with a knotted rope which is to beat Him, and ends up dramatically with a clenched fist about to fall on His face.

Dürer. The dancing peasants. Victoria & Albert Museum, London

30

Besides this main rhythm, many smaller rhythms run through the picture, creating a rich interplay of movement which gives the composition a strong vitality.

In an earlier example of Mondrian's painting we said that his aim was to entertain the eye in the same way as music entertains the ear. Again we have an example of his work in which he is using flat areas of colour to suggest the music of jazz. The eye creates its own rhythm in this picture, as it leaps from colour to colour. The small black oblongs seem to do a separate little dance of their own, whilst the large areas of blue, orange and red form continually-changing patterns which lead the eye in a jerking dance. Although the areas of colour are actually painted on the surface, Mondrian, using his knowledge of colour, has made some appear to come forward and others to go back. In this way the rhythm is made in and out of the canvas as well as over the surface of it.

Mondrian. Composition 1917. Rijksmuseum Kröller-Müller, Otterlo

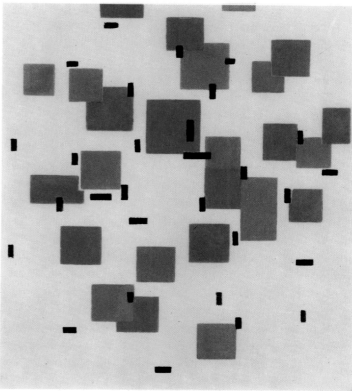

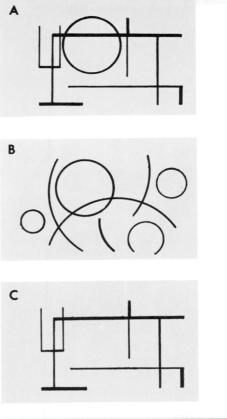

echoes in composition

A good composition should be pleasing to the eye: no part of it should look out of place or be unrelated to the rest of the composition.

By using *echoes* in his composition, an artist can relate all the different parts of his picture so that each bears some resemblance to the other, and a pleasing whole is achieved.

Look at these three diagrams. The first (A) shows several lines and a circle arranged in a rectangle. The circle is instantly obvious, and looks very much 'out of place', because there is no other shape in the composition similar to its own.

Diagram (B) shows the same circle in exactly the same position in the rectangle, but this time surrounded by other circles and curved lines. Here the similar shapes and lines echo one another and form quite a pleasant composition.

Diagram (C) shows the same arrangement of straight lines as in the first diagram, only this time the circle has been removed. Here again the composition feels pleasant because all the different parts of the composition echo one another.

We have already seen how artists use the straight lines of triangles, verticals or horizontals to give a good structure to their compositions. In fact, one of the reasons why artists so often use straight lines in their pictures is because a straight line echoes the side of the canvas or frame.

The picture by Madox Brown, the English artist, is painted on an almost circular canvas, and its composition is made up of circular lines and rhythms without a single straight line in it.

Now consider this picture of the Crucifixion by Raphael, the Italian painter. The picture was originally intended for a church, and the shape of the canvas he painted on was determined by the church architecture. The canvas had to be square at the bottom, and semi-circular at the top, rather like church windows. Here was a double problem for the painter to face. He had to construct a composition which would echo both a circle and a square at the same time!

Raphael based his picture on a composition which does this very thing. First of all he built a triangle of three straight lines at the bottom of the picture, as you can see in the diagram. The top of the triangle is at

Giovanni Bellini. Madonna with two saints. Academy, Venice

Madox Brown. The last of England. Fitzwilliam Museum, Cambridge

32

Raphael. Crucifixion. National Gallery, London

Christ's face, and its sides run through the heads of the kneeling figures and down their backs. In this way a stable triangle forms the link between the three main figures. Not content merely to echo the sides of the canvas with these three lines, he made them the same length as the straight sides of the frame. Whilst echoing the bottom of the frame, the triangle serves to echo and support the upside-down triangle of the Cross.

His next problem was to find something which would relate the circular top to the rest of the design. For this purpose he made use of two circles. He placed the top of one circle at the apex of the triangle, adding further emphasis to the subject of the picture. Using Christ's knee as the centre point, he drew a circle which linked together six of the important features of the painting — the chalice held by the angels and the faces of the four people standing at the foot of the cross. His next circle is just as obvious, passing through Christ's nailed feet and the two feet of the angels, almost through Christ's nailed hands, and across the inscription at the top. In this way he not only echoes the upper curve of the frame, but at the same time makes a connecting thread between all the people in the picture.

We can see from this picture that Raphael was one of the world's finest artists and a complete master of picture design and composition.

33

Paul Klee. They're biting. Tate Gallery, London

guesswork and certainty

When Raphael painted his picture of the Crucifixion he worked out exactly where everything in his picture should be. There was a definite reason why he placed Christ's head in that particular place on the canvas. There was a definite reason for the angels' positions in the air, and for the placing of the people around the foot of the cross. His composition was based on a thorough reasoning, and nothing was left to chance.

However, not all artists organise their compositions in the same mathematical way. Instead of working out in advance how the picture should be painted, some artists rely on their own taste and judgment as they paint. Instead of using strict rules they paint them in a way which 'feels' right to them.

A good example of this sort of painting is the picture by Paul Klee of a man fishing. Klee is interested in painting a picture which would have a quality similar to a fairy story. We all like stories of knights, giants and dwarfs—and we probably enjoy just as much the cartoon films of Donald Duck, Bugs Bunny or Tom and Jerry—but we don't believe that these creatures and animals actually exist. In mediaeval days many hand-written books were decorated with funny, grotesque and quite unreal animals. The two strange little creatures on this page would live in a very different world from the one we know. They are 'make believe' and quite unreal, but we enjoy looking at them.

This is what Klee is aiming at in his picture—he wants to create an unreal little world which we can look at and enjoy. The strange man is not very realistically drawn, nor would his fishing line be much use in real life. As for the fish, they are pure imagination and quite unlike real fish. The whole painting is a half-humorous but very beautiful 'fairy story' in paint.

Klee's composition is not in the least organised in the sense that Raphael's picture was organised. For this picture he has relied entirely on his own special sense of placing for the positions of everything he has drawn, and yet everything is perfectly arranged. Take the sun, for instance: there is no reason why it should be in that particular position, yet it feels just right. So does the quaint little boat which floats on this improbable little pond. There is no apparent reason why the exclamation mark should be in the middle of the water—yet take it out and the picture looks strangely empty.

When an artist, like Klee, uses his 'feelings' instead of reasoning, he is said to be using his *intuition*. Intuition

Pisanello. The vision of St Eustace. National Gallery, London

is really the emotions, or feelings, making a judgment, whereas reasoning is the mind, or intellect, making a judgment. Thus, when an artist uses his intuition in designing he is simply doing something which 'feels right' but for which he can give no definite reason.

The picture by Pisanello of animals in a dark wood (The Vision of St Eustace) was painted over 500 years before Klee's fishing scene, yet it shows the same sort of intuitive composition. Each separate animal is placed as it is because Pisanello *felt* that it should go in that position. There is no basic composition of carefully worked-out structures, yet the painting is very pleasant to look at because the balance is sound.

It is interesting to see that both Klee and Pisanello used the same device for linking together all the different subjects of their pictures. In each painting the background colouring is almost the same throughout the picture area, and this helps to create a unity. Look, for instance, at the drawing of the Pisanello without the dark background. It is 'bitty' and unorganised. This gives some idea of how important a link the background colouring is in the composition.

geometry and art

Paintings and sculpture have different effects on different people. What some people like, others may well dislike, and we all have our own particular ideas about what is beautiful.

Yet, in spite of this, men throughout the ages have searched for ways of producing works of art which would appear beautiful to everyone. They have searched for laws of beauty as exact as the laws of mathematics. If we add two and two we always get four—this is mathematics—and some artists have wanted an art just as certain and exact as this. They have wanted to be able to arrange lines, shapes and colours in a way that would appear beautiful to everyone who looked at them.

We have already seen that a good framework is a basis for a good painting, and that such a framework is made out of simple shapes like triangles and circles—out of geometry, in fact. If these basic geometric shapes were ugly in themselves, the pictures could hardly be expected to be beautiful. Artists saw this very clearly, and began to experiment with such shapes, to see how and why they were beautiful. As geometry is part of mathematics, they were looking at the basic mathematics behind art.

If an artist is basing the composition of a picture on one single triangle, he can make it much more interesting by moving its apex over to one side. Obviously, exactly how far the top of the triangle is moved over is of great importance. If we move it too far over to one side, it will overbalance and be no good for a composition. If we don't move it enough, it will be boring and equally useless for a composition. It must be moved so that it feels just right. Rembrandt did this very successfully, because his sense of placing was so good.

Many artists were not content to arrange compositions just because they 'felt right': they wanted to know *why* they felt right. They found that if they placed the subject of their pictures in a certain position on their canvas, this position tended to look considerably better than any other.

Here we have two compositions which have the centre of interest at the same point on the canvas. In the painting by Turner, of Norham Castle, which is almost swimming in light and atmosphere, the animal is placed to the right of the composition. The first thing to catch our attention in this picture of an industrial town by Lowry is the dark mill on the right.

36

Turner. Norham Castle at sunrise. Tate Gallery, London
Lowry. The pond. Tate Gallery, London

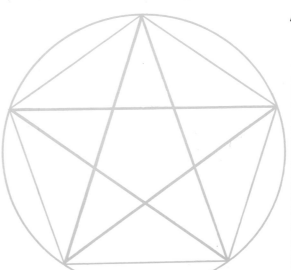

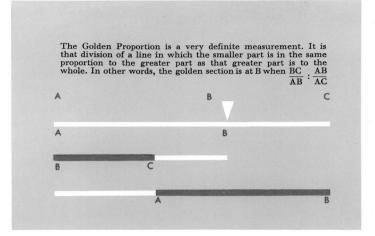

The Golden Proportion is a very definite measurement. It is that division of a line in which the smaller part is in the same proportion to the greater part as that greater part is to the whole. In other words, the golden section is at B when $\frac{BC}{AB} : \frac{AB}{AC}$

This is one of the many fascinating designs which can be made by using the golden section. The smaller half of each proportion is again divided at the golden section along its longest side. This produces a sort of 'spiral of squares'.

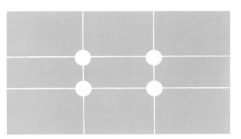

If you draw a vertical line through the centre of the subject in these two pictures, you will find that they cut the top and bottom in exactly the same place. The top of the picture, in each case, is divided into two lines which have the same proportion.

This proportion is well known in the world of art, and is called the *Golden Section*, or the Golden Proportion. It is a definite proportion which can be measured or constructed with rule and compass. The diagrams show how to construct the golden proportion, and how to find the golden section of a given line.

This section can, of course, be found on either side of a line, to the left or to the right. If we find the golden section on the sides of a rectangle, and draw perpendiculars through them, we shall have the golden proportion of the rectangle itself. From the diagram you will see that it is possible to find four points within the rectangle where the golden sections cut each other. These four points are good places to put the centre of interest of a picture. They are points where the subject of a painting looks well placed.

Both Turner and Lowry used one of these points as the position for their main subject. Perhaps they didn't work out with geometry or mathematics where to place their subjects, but did so by feeling alone. But whatever their method, they did place their main centre of interest at the same point as some other artist might by using geometry itself.

We can see now that the most satisfying position for the apex of a triangle is linked up with the golden section. A perpendicular line from the apex to the base should cut the base at the golden mean. Very many portrait paintings are based on precisely this sort of triangular composition.

To find the length of extension required on a given line AB in order to form a golden proportion with that line. Drop a perpendicular from B to C, so that BC = AB. With compass at ½AB draw a large arc cutting a line extended from AB at D. $\frac{BD}{AB} : \frac{AB}{AD}$

To find the Golden Section of a given line AB. Draw a perpendicular at B and mark off along this perpendicular ½AB at C. Join AC, and with compass at A cut AC at D so that AD also equals ½AB. With compass at C measure off length CD. With compass radius DC and centre A, cut AB at E. $\frac{EB}{AE} : \frac{AE}{AB}$

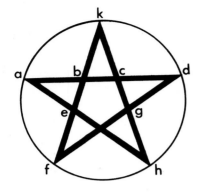

As you can see, the various proportions of the lines on a pentagram inscribed within a circle are all exactly based on the golden mean.

e.g.— $\dfrac{BC}{AB} : \dfrac{AB}{AC} : \dfrac{CD}{AC} : \dfrac{AC}{AD}$ etc.

Canon and proportion in Egyptian art, British Museum

seashells and drinking cups

The Ancient Egyptians were the first to use mathematics in art. They discovered many interesting proportions, among them the golden section, and began to use them in their buildings and works of art. The illustration shows how the Egyptians carefully worked out the geometry and proportions for their wall-paintings. The Pyramids and certain tomb monuments, as well as a few of the immense statues, are built with the golden proportion as the basis for their beauty.

Legend has it that the Greek mathematician Eudoxos, who lived some 350 years before Christ, was the first man to try to find out why the golden section was so pleasing. He is said to have gone around with a long stick, asking his friends to mark it at any point they found the most interesting or pleasing. He was astonished to find that the majority of people agreed almost exactly as to where the point should be. It was at the Golden Section.

Eudoxos worked out the mathematics of the golden proportion, and found that it was a number which could be expressed by a formula. The formula for the golden proportion was called PHI after Phidias, an artist, who used the golden proportion a great deal in his sculpture.

Pythagoras, the Greek geometer, became especially interested in the formula, and suspected that it was the basis for the proportions of the human figure. This he proved to be correct, and showed that the human body is built with each part in a definite golden proportion to all the other parts.

The Greeks found that with only the golden section as a basis, it is possible to make many wonderful designs and shapes. These form excellent geometric compositions for paintings because of their mathematical exactness. One such shape is a pentagram (which is a regular five-sided figure). In this diagram you can see that all the lines are closely related to each other by the golden proportion. This five-pointed star became very popular with artists in their compositions—particularly in Italy during the Renaissance. Further study showed that this proportion was the basis for many natural forms, such as shells, snowflakes, plants, etc.

These discoveries had a tremendous effect on Greek Art. Painters, sculptors and potters began to construct their works on the principle of the golden proportion. This Greek drinking cup, for example, was made with the section as its basic proportion, and practically all good Greek vases were constructed in a similar mathematical way. You should by now be able to see the many

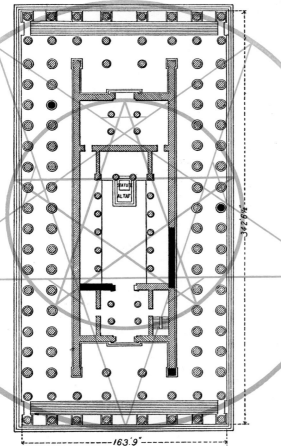

Temple of Diana, Ephesus (ground plan)

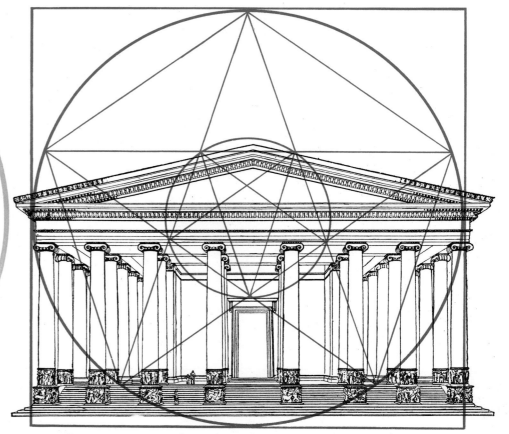

Temple of Diana, Ephesus (front elevation)

The Parthenon on the Acropolis, Athens. J. Allan Cash

Greek kylix, 480 B.C. British Museum

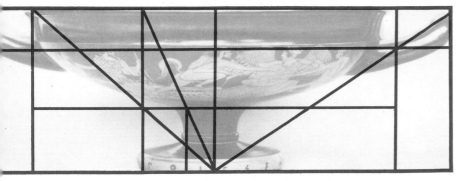

golden proportions on the analysis of the Greek cup.

But it was in architecture, above all the other arts, that the Greeks employed the theories of the golden section. Every part of their major buildings from the general shape down to the smallest detail of decoration were constructed upon this proportion. The two diagrams above are of the Greek Temple of Diana at Ephesus, which is no longer in existence. Both the interior and exterior were designed to fit within a pentagram. The Parthenon, a temple at Athens, was perhaps the best example of this mathematical approach to art. The whole effect of this building must have been magnificent, but unfortunately it is now in ruins. Most of the roof and the entire back was completely destroyed when a store of ammunition, kept there by the Turks, exploded in the year 1687.

39

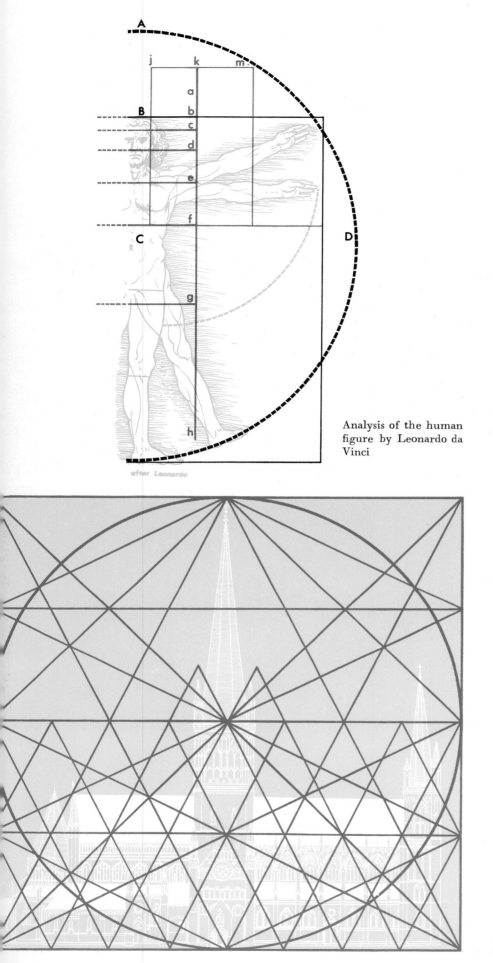

Analysis of the human figure by Leonardo da Vinci

after Leonardo

the divine proportion

The Mediaeval builders of churches and cathedrals approached the design of their buildings in much the same way as the Greeks. A good geometric structure was their aim. Inside and out, their buildings were intricate constructions based on the golden proportion.

They used this proportion not merely because it was beautiful to look at, but because they believed that it came from God. So many things in nature, from the human body down to the smallest plants, were living examples of the laws of the golden section that they believed that it must be a law made by God. Like Dante, the Italian poet, they believed that 'Nature is the art of God', and that the golden section, playing such an important part in it, must be an expression of His purpose. It was for this reason that they called it the 'mystic proportion'.

This drawing of a Mediaeval Cathedral shows something of the lengths to which these architects would go in order to mirror and express their understanding of God's laws and purpose. It is built entirely on a foundation of geometry in which the golden section plays an important part.

But whilst in architecture there was this very great interest in geometry, painting seemed to have lost all interest in the golden proportion, and in mathematics as a whole. It was not until the fifteenth century, in Italy, that artists found a renewed interest in geometry. Perhaps the greatest of these Italian artists was Piero della Francesca, who painted pictures of a very obvious geometric nature. This picture by him comes from a wall in an Italian palace. Its subject is the flagellation, or beating, of Christ, but how different an approach it is from the one by Grünewald, which was so full of rhythms and vitality. This is certainly a geometric art.

Analysis of Nidaros Cathedral, after McCody Lund.
After 'Ad Quadratum' by kind permission of Batsford Press

40

Piero della Francesca. The flagellation. Ducal Palace, Urbino

'without measurement, there can be no art.'

Francesca had a great influence on Luca Paccioli, another Italian, who wrote a book on the golden section which he called the 'divine proportion'. He too thought that the proportion came from God, and taught that 'without measurement, there can be no art'.

The book, published in 1509, was illustrated by no less an artist than Leonardo da Vinci, and contained many of the collected theories about the golden proportion. Leonardo had for a long time been interested in the mathematics of art and nature. He had earlier, like Pythagoras, made a close study of the human figure and had shown how all its different parts were related by the golden section.

The discoveries of men like Francesca, Paccioli and Leonardo had an enormous effect on Italian art, particularly on painting, and artists once more began to construct their compositions on the golden proportion.

You will remember that we saw how Raphael had constructed a very fine composition for his 'Crucifixion' from two circles and a triangle. If you look more closely at the picture, you will see that in fact he used a pentagram in the uppermost circle, and two pentagrams in the lower circle. Each point of these three stars touches some important part of the composition, and creates an incredibly rich mathematical design based on the golden proportion. The two long sides of the large triangle which holds the picture together are related to the base by the golden proportion. Thus we find that the whole of the picture is not merely a clever arrangement of two circles and a triangle—it is an exact geometric construction deliberately based on the mathematics of the golden proportion.

Many artists since the Italian Renaissance have been actively interested in geometric painting. Among these, one of the greatest was Piet Mondrian, who died in 1944. His style of painting was based on a severe geommetry, and has had a great effect on modern art.

Raphael. Crucifixion. National Gallery, London

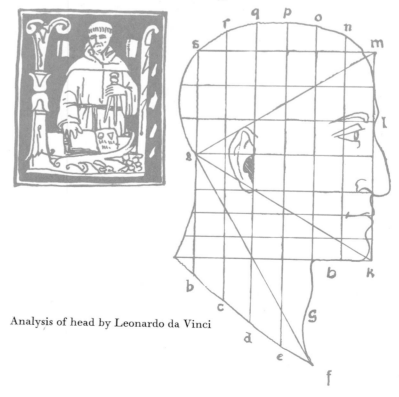

Analysis of head by Leonardo da Vinci

Nicholson. Painting. Tate Gallery, London

Mondrian. Painting in blue and yellow.
National Gallery of Art, Washington, D.C.

43

'as I can, but not as I would.'

If you look carefully at the reflection in the mirror, you will see the great artist Jan Van Eyck himself. Palette in hand, and assistant by his side, he is painting the portrait of Jan Arnolfini, a rich Flemish merchant, and his new bride. This is the year 1434, when marriages were not recorded by certificates, as they are now. Arnolfini has asked Van Eyck to paint this picture as a record of his marriage. In this way, Van Eyck is acting as a kind of 'best man', and this he makes plain with his signature 'Jan Van Eyck was here in 1434.'

From the picture you can see that Arnolfini is making a sign of his marriage vow with his right hand, whilst taking his new wife with his left. This is an important moment—a religious vow is being made. In order to make the importance of the moment clear, Van Eyck has included many religious *symbols* in the painting. The terrier dog, for instance, is a 15th century symbol of Faith. The rosary hanging on the wall is a symbol of their Church. One candle, burning in a room which is already full of light, is a symbol of Hope. Two pairs of shoes lying on the floor are to remind us of the Biblical text, 'Put off thy shoes from off thy feet, for the place whereon thou standest is holy ground'.

Van Eyck has spared himself no pains to make this his masterpiece. Not only the detail is perfect, but the composition behind the painting is well constructed.

Notice how Arnolfini's face, which is the most important feature in the picture, is given emphasis. First it is given importance by being a light area surrounded by the dark shape of the immense hat. Then, secondly, with the aid of the clever pointers (A) both in the background and in the foreground, it is further emphasised.

The balance of the picture is interesting. Van Eyck has created each figure in its own space, much like a gothic window (B), and has linked the two together in the middle of the picture. Since this is a painting to record a wedding—the joining together of two people —the linking of the man and woman in the middle of the picture is very appropriate.

The composition itself is worth close study. The two figures are enclosed within triangular forms, with the faces almost at the top. Notice how Van Eyck ingeniously varies these triangles so as to avoid boredom by too much repetition. Perhaps the most original device in the composition is the use of a circular band, marked in red on the picture. Within this area he has placed the hands and faces of the two people, creating a beau-

Jan van Eyck. Arnolfini and his wife. National Gallery, London

tiful circular rhythm which is repeated many times in the painting as an echo, uniting the background and the foreground.

Almost nothing is known about Jan Van Eyck, except that he died in 1441. But a sign of the humility of this great master is his personal motto: 'Als ikh kan!', which is part of a Flemish proverb meaning: 'As I can, but not as I would'. The painting is the best he can do, but not as good as he would wish it to be!

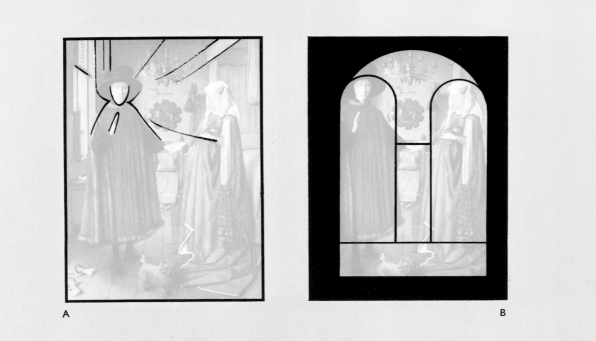

A   B

Detail of mirror from Jan van Eyck's Arnolfini and his wife

pattern in design

A good design is one which gives just the right emphasis to all the different parts in it. The aim of an artist is to link up the lines, shapes and colours in his composition just enough to make a pleasing picture. When he succeeds in doing this, his picture is said to be in *harmony*.

Harmony depends on a unity in the different things which make up a composition or design. We have seen, for instance, that an artist uses lines of a similar kind to echo one another in his composition. This creates a unity without which there could be no harmony.

One of the ways an artist can bring unity and harmony into his painting is with the use of pattern. The word 'pattern' really has two meanings. It can mean a definite shape, or it can mean a design made by a repetition of a shape.

This lovely portrait of a lady by Baldovinetti is a profile shape which might be called a pattern. At the same time, the three flowers embroidered on her dress are also patterns.

When a pattern is made from the repetition of a shape, that shape is said to be the *motif* for the pattern. You have often seen how wallpaper design is formed by the repetition of one small picture or shape—this picture or shape is the motif for the pattern. Such motifs can be taken from nature, like a flower or an animal, or they can be based on some abstract shape, like a square or a dot.

The quality of line is a very important part of design. Perhaps the main thing about the portrait by Baldovinetti, which makes it such a lovely picture, is the way in which the pattern of the lady has been drawn against the background. Everywhere along this line there are curves. There are large curves and small curves, all put together to make a wonderful pattern which covers the whole of the picture area.

Picasso's painting of a young lady has similar points of pattern interest. The lady is looking in the same direction and is seen in profile. Here, however, Picasso has used straight lines to build up the outline, instead of curves. Nonetheless, he creates a pattern outline just as beautiful and exciting as the one which appears in Baldovinetti's picture.

Notice how, in both pictures, the quality of line is continued into the patterned shape. Baldovinetti uses curved lines for the drawing within the pattern, whilst Picasso uses straight lines. A good pattern depends on its outline, which must have a certain unity about it.

Baldovinetti. Portrait of a lady in yellow. National Gallery, London

'The Umbrellas', by the French painter Renoir, has a wonderful pattern 'theme' of echoing curves and rhythms. The motif for the pattern seems to be a simple curve, such as can be seen on the umbrellas, and it is echoed almost everywhere within the picture. We can see a similar unity of pattern shape in the little drawing of Greeks running. Notice how the artist has tried to create a unity, even in the shapes formed between the arms and bodies inside the pattern formed by the group of figures.

Renoir. The umbrellas. (Lane bequest) National Gallery, London (on loan to Municipal Gallery of Modern Art, Dublin)

Picasso. Portrait of a young woman. Private collection.

Persian rug. 19th century. Victoria & Albert Museum, London

Holbein. Jane Seymour. Kunsthistorisches Museum, Vienna

square carpets and round tables

Patterns can be very simple or very complex. They can be as simple as dots on a girl's frock, or as complicated as the designs on some carpets. But however simple or complicated they may be, they are always built up on the principle of one part being the basis for the whole pattern.

Painters make use of pattern in their pictures to create a sense of unity. Obviously, if the whole picture is built up from similar smaller units, then that picture will have a certain unity and harmony. Such harmony will depend on similarity of shapes.

Here we have a picture by Holbein of Jane Seymour, the third wife of Henry VIII. There are three basic shapes for the pattern which is built on three motifs: one which is semi-circular, one which has four sides, and one which is a small round shape. In this way a pattern unity is created over the whole of the picture. Try for yourself to find these three motifs, and to see how they are evenly distributed over the picture area.

The desire to create a pattern unity sometimes leads an artist to distort the appearance of the things he is painting. The picture by the French artist Bonnard is a very good example of this intentional distortion. The two basic pattern shapes in this painting are the square and the circle. The door, table and baskets form the squares, whilst the plates, dishes and the lady's head form the circles.

48

Bonnard. The table. Tate Gallery, London © S.P.A.D.E.M. PARIS 1963

Now separately the square and circle are very good simple motifs to use, but together they are difficult. Their shapes do not form a unity: there is no similarity of shape or feeling between the straight sides of the square and the curves of the circle.

Bonnard knew this, and solved the problem by making the straight lines of the squares slightly curved and by making the circles slightly square!

See how the dishes and plates on the table are made to fit more into a square than into a circle, as we know they should do. Notice also how the corners of the table have been cleverly rounded off, to give it a circular shape. One corner is cut off by the picture frame; the next is cut off by the basket of oranges and the silver milk jug, and the corner where the woman is sitting is linked up with her arm, thus giving a rounded edge instead of a sharp corner. The bottom left corner is perfectly square, but Bonnard uses it to echo the square edge of the picture.

On the table itself, Bonnard makes clever use of the shadows to destroy the circular shapes of the dishes. The basket with a few oranges in it, for instance, is made almost into a square by the shadow. Similarly with the two large plates. The basket in the foreground is given a more circular shape by the shadow below it. This same shadow is cast in such a way that it destroys the straight edge of the table, which would be too much of a straight line in this picture.

All this distortion of natural shapes—of turning squares into circles and circles into squares—produces a wonderful unity of pattern in the picture.

49

black lines and circuses

Pattern has been used in painting since the beginning of history. The Ancient Egyptians had a tendency to mark out their pattern shapes clearly with lines. This method has come into vogue again in recent times— Toulouse-Lautrec, the French painter, employed it with great success at the end of the last century. The lines used by the Egyptians were usually continuous and of more or less the same thickness; and tended to make the patterns a little more stiff. They were therefore suitable for the religious wall-paintings in tombs and temples. The lines used by Lautrec are broken and of varying thicknesses. Such broken lines give a strong sense of vitality, or urgency, to the pattern shape. In this particular painting, of course, they are intended to suggest the brisk movement of the circus

When bounding lines become very thick, they themselves begin to play a part in the design. The picture by Rouault, also a French painter, is built out of thick black lines—almost slabs of black—which give added colour brightness to the pattern shapes. Paintings of this sort are sometimes called *cloisonné* (pronounced clwasonay) after the French word meaning 'partitioned off', because each of the colours is separated by the black partition lines. Stained glass is a good example of *cloisonné* work. In stained glass, however, the black lines are actually pieces of lead which not only separate the pieces of glass, but also hold them together.

When a picture is painted in a realistic way it loses much of its pattern. Courbet's picture is very lovely to look at: the details of the apples and the wonderful way he has painted the light and shade is a delight. But his picture has not got the same pattern interest as the ones by Sutherland and Braque. Courbet's apples feel solid and weighty—we can almost pick them up and eat them—but because he has been interested in making them look fairly realistic, he has had to lose much of their pattern shapes.

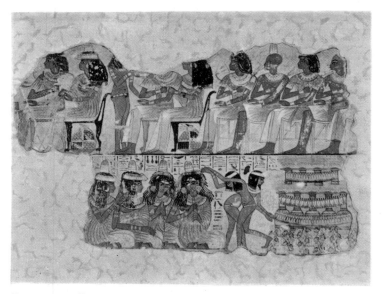

Egyptian wall-painting. Banqueting scene. British Museum

Rouault. Heads of two clowns. Norbert Schimmel Collection

50

Sutherland. Still life with gourds. Collection of Mrs Moreland

Braque. Still life with tablecloth. Museum of Modern Art, Paris

Courbet. Still life. National Gallery, London

Lautrec. Cirque Fernando: the ringmaster. Joseph
Winterbotham Collection, Art Institute, Chicago

Chagall. Artist with model. National Gallery of Canada, Ottawa

Vermeer. The artist in his studio. Kunsthistorisches Museum, Vienna

ideas and meanings

A symbol is anything which is used to pass on an idea or meaning.

Words are symbols because they are used to pass on thoughts and ideas. Pictures are also symbols because they can communicate feelings and meanings. The meanings and feelings behind these two pictures are very different, but they both have the same subject—an artist painting a model. The Dutch artist Vermeer painted himself in his own studio, surrounded with beautiful things. It is a calm, peaceful and lovely scene. When the modern artist Chagall painted himself and a model, he wanted to convey something of the intense emotion which goes into the creation of a work of art. He wanted also to pass on the idea of the strange, imaginative world of the artist—a world of a dreamlike nature, where the real and the unreal are mixed. The real world he symbolises by himself and his model, the unreal world of imagination by the head of the blue ass and by the strange bird-like creature in the sky.

You will remember that when Van Eyck wanted to represent Faith in his wedding picture he drew a terrier dog at the couple's feet. This type of dog was well known to the Flemish people of that time for its great loyalty and devotion to its master, so Van Eyck could use it to stand for Faith. The dog was a symbol of Faith. Van Eyck couldn't paint Faith itself, because it has no appearance, so he had to use something to stand for it.

The Australian native who scratched those marks on a piece of wood said that they were 'kangaroos'. They probably did convey the idea of kangaroos to him, because he understood the meaning of the symbol he was drawing.

If we look at the words we use, we shall understand how an abstract mark, like a letter, can pass on a meaning. The word DOG is an arrangement of three letters of the alphabet—it is not a dog in itself. The word DOG cannot run about wagging a tail, but it can pass on the idea of the animal which can do these things. DGO does not mean anything at all, and is therefore not a symbol. Nor does ODG mean anything. GOD means something entirely different. DOG means something because people have agreed that these three letters, spelt in that order, mean dog.

We couldn't understand at first what the wiggly line cut on to the piece of wood meant—it didn't look in the least *like* a kangaroo. We can see now, though, that the Australian native wouldn't understand our word-

symbol KANGAROO, unless, of course, he could speak or read English!

Sometimes it is possible to have a symbol meaning two things at once. In Rome, in the early days of Christianity, it was against the law to worship God or to speak about Christ. But as the Christians wanted to speak about Christ to each other, without the Roman soldiers knowing, they decided to use a symbol to stand for Him. This symbol they chose to be a fish; and it was adopted for a very definite reason.

The following sentence in Greek means 'Jesus Christ, Son of God, Saviour': Ιησους Χριστὸς Θεου Υζὸς Σωτήρ.

If you take the first letter of each of these Greek words you get ἰχθύs —ichthus—which is the Greek word for fish. By using this word, or a picture of a fish, they were able to talk about Christ whilst the enemies of Christianity thought they were talking about fish!

Look at these pictures of an owl. One was drawn 20 years ago, the other 200 years ago, whilst the coin was made in Greece over 2,000 years ago. They all mean exactly the same thing in spite of their different styles. They all represent the same thing.

A few hundred years ago many men believed that it was possible to make gold out of lead and they made very many experiments to try to discover the secret. They were called alchemists, and in order to guard their secrets they invented and used special symbols to stand for certain ideas. Many of the meanings contained in these symbols have since been lost, and we are left only with the symbols themselves. This woodcut of a lion eating the sun is an alchemical symbol.

IXΘYE

Bewick. Owl.
Author's collection

Picasso. Owl. From
'Poems and Lithographs'
published by the
Louis Leiris Gallery

Athenian coin, 5th century.
British Museum

Athenian vase, 5th century. British Museum

ships and trees

When an artist draws something he uses line. He draws the outline of a thing, and uses line to indicate what is inside the outline.

But such lines do not exist in nature. A line is just one of the ways of representing a thing's shape so that we can recognise it. Thus a drawing is a special sort of symbol used to convey meanings and ideas.

An artist looks at nature, and at life around him, and translates the things he sees into symbols. All painting and all sculpture deals with the arranging of symbols in a particular way.

Here are two drawings of ships. They are both symbols. The first was drawn in the eleventh century, and shows St Guthlac being carried to an island in a small boat. Notice how the waves have been drawn—not at all realistically. The wavy lines are not at all like real waves or water—they are symbols. The tree to the right of the picture is a symbol of a tree, which is placed there to indicate that there is land ahead.

St Guthlac and his two companions are too big for the small boat. In real life they would sink into the waves. But the mediaeval artist who drew them regarded them as being the most important part of the picture, so he made them larger then they should be to emphasise their importance. The drawing of St Guthlac could be of any man, but to make the symbol quite definite and clear in our minds, the artist has written 'St Guthlac' above his head!

The boat is very simply drawn; it is just a flat pattern without anything in its design which makes it a special kind of boat. It is a symbol of any boat.

But if you look at this *woodcut* done in the sixteenth century you will see that it is of a very special ship. It is a picture of the 'Ark Royal' which was the flagship of Queen Elizabeth I. Because it was a special ship, the artist was anxious to convey as much information about it as possible. Each rope, mast and flag is seen in the greatest detail. The sea is drawn in almost the same way as the sea in our other picture; and the little boy in the cloud at top left is very clearly meant to be a symbol of the wind, to show its direction. The ship is itself a symbol—but unlike the other little boat, it is a symbol of one particular and important ship.

In his attempt to show all the details of the ship the

The entry into Jerusalem, French, 13th century. British Museum

Guthlac Roll. St. Guthlac being rowed to Crowland. British Museum

Woodcut of the Ark Royal, 16th century. British Museum

54

Constable. Salisbury Cathedral. Victoria & Albert Museum, London

artist has drawn many different parts in a special way. He has not drawn them realistically, but has altered the natural appearance of things to convey certain ideas. The side of the ship, for instance, is seen in profile, as if she is sailing straight past us—yet we can also see the back, as if she is sailing away from us. This is a similar way of altering facts as in the first picture, where the three men are drawn several sizes too large to show their importance. Both artists have departed from what they know to be fact in order to emphasise something they consider to be important. They have used a special sort of symbolism called *distortion*.

What we call 'realistic' painting is still symbolical. Perhaps these two paintings will make this point clear. The first is a mediaeval picture of Christ's entry into Jerusalem. The tree in this painting does not pretend to be very realistic. Each group of leaves is symbolised by a round ball at the top of a branch. The artist has made no attempt to draw in each leaf, and the trunk of the tree is the same colour as the leaves. The painting is very clearly a symbol of a tree.

The trees in Constable's picture of Salisbury Cathedral appear at first sight to be very realistic. But if you look closely at them you will see that each leaf is painted in the same way—despite the fact that in reality each leaf has a distinct shape of its own. This painting, though naturalistic, is still as much a symbol as the mediaeval tree, but the trees go much nearer to representing a woodland as it appears to our eyes.

We all know that if we look at a tree from a distance the leaves look like a large mass. If we go a little closer they take on an individual shape, and we can see their 'veins' under the green skin. If we examine such a leaf under a microscope we see fine hair-like threads and pores. No artist, however clever, could put all this into his painting. He has to stop at some point in his attempt to copy appearance. He can't paint everything he sees and knows to be there. He must select certain things from reality to use as his symbols. Exactly what he selects determines the meaning and nature of his picture.

Henry Lamb. Lamentation (detail). Tate Gallery, London

Picasso. Crying woman. Roland Penrose Collection

distortion

Compare these two pictures of women crying. One is a detail of a painting by the English artist Henry Lamb, and the other is by Picasso. The painting by Lamb is very realistic: you can see very clearly from her face how she is suffering. It is a straightforward picture of how a woman looks when she weeps.

Picasso's picture, however, goes a little deeper—he is not content merely to present the outward appearance of a crying face; he wants to convey the inner suffering. His painting is of the suffering in the woman's mind, rather than of her face. From the picture one can almost feel her agonies and despair.

To convey a particular feeling Picasso has distorted the natural appearance of the face. Lamb didn't distort his picture very much—but he didn't succeed in pass-

ing on the sense of suffering that Picasso did. Lamb conveys more the *idea* of someone crying, whilst Picasso conveys the idea and the *feeling* of someone crying.

When an artist distorts or exaggerates the natural appearance of a thing to express some feeling or other, he is said to be painting in an *expressionist* style. Expressionism passes on ideas and strong feelings by means of distortion.

Grünewald, who painted this altarpiece of Christ crucified, was an expressionist. If you look closely at the figures—particularly at the hands of Christ—you will see how well he distorted the natural appearance of things in order to pass on a deep feeling of the agony and suffering at the Crucifixion.

Detail from Eisenheim altar-piece

Grünewald. Eisenheim altar-piece

Henry Lamb. Lamentation. Tate Gallery, London

light in painting

An artist gets all his ideas for paintings from the world around him—and this world is flooded with light. It seems hardly surprising, therefore, that light should fascinate artists.

Toward the end of the last century, a group of French painters set out to record the appearance of the world as they saw it. They wanted to paint a scene as it would appear to a person who opened his eyes for only a second or two, rather like the shutters of cameras. Of course, what a person sees—his impressions—depends on the light, so in fact these artists were painting light. This group of painters became known as *Impressionists*.

It was Claude Monet who was the unquestioned leader of the movement. Indeed, the new style received its name from a Monet painting entitled *Impression*, first shown in 1874. He observed that the same subject looks quite different at different times of the day. The sun moves, and the light changes, thus altering the appearance of things. In order to catch the different effects of light throughout a day, he would spend the whole day painting very many pictures of a scene. For one of his subjects he chose a haystack, and painted some fifteen pictures in one day—all of which were amazingly different to look at, even though of the same object. Monet said that he made this experiment in order to get a true impression of a certain aspect of nature as he saw it, and not as he knew it in fact to be.

Of course, light changes very quickly through the course of one day, and Monet knew that if he were to paint one haystack all day long, he would be painting it with many different light effects, and would have to paint quickly. Poor Monet had quite a difficult time, for as he said, 'the sun sets so fast I can hardly follow it!'

Degas's picture of the ballet girls is more a study of light falling evenly over a room, than of figures in action. Another impressionist was Seurat. Besides being a painter he was also interested in science, and had read much of what scientists thought about light. He found

Monet. Haystack at Giverny. Museum of Fine Arts, Boston
© S.P.A.D.E.M. PARIS 1963

light from the sun can be split up into several distinct pure colours. This was done with the aid of the spectrum, and the effect was to produce a small rainbow. Seurat was fascinated by such experiments, and tried painting pictures with small dabs of pure colour.

When his pictures are looked at from a distance these dabs and dots of colour merge into one another, and form a rich feeling of lively colour. Because of the way Seurat and his friends used small points of colour, they were called *Pointillistes*.

What the Impressionists and Pointillistes discovered was what Rembrandt knew a long time before them— that light is colour: that you can only paint light with the use of colour.

Degas. The rehearsal. Glasgow Art Gallery   © S.P.A.D.E.M. PARIS 1963

Seurat. Bathing at Asnières. National Gallery, London

Detail from Bathing at Asnières

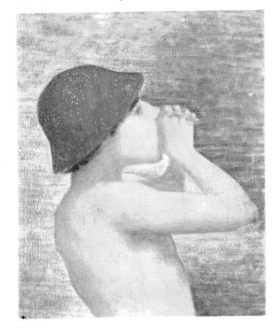

Turner. Norham Castle at sunrise. Tate Gallery, London

turner and nature

Joseph Mallard William Turner was perhaps the greatest of English painters, and is considered one of the world's great painters of light and atmosphere. He was born near Covent Garden, in London, on April 23rd, 1775. At an early age, when he was about thirteen, he began to earn his living by drawing and painting scenes of churches and towns, as well as local beauty spots. He even became quite popular as a painter in this way, and was elected to the Royal Academy.

Gradually, however, his style changed, and people who had praised him before could no longer understand what he was trying to paint. He had, in fact, begun to paint light and movement in a new and startling way. Friends and critics who were not accustomed to his new way of looking at nature thought that he had gone mad, and he was accused of making 'pictures of nothing and very like'. His accusers said of him much as people say of many artists today: that he was not looking closely at nature, that he was not finishing his pictures properly, and that he was painting in blots and streaks!

But Turner took no notice of what people said, and continued to paint. His subject was Nature and light, and these two things he studied intently. Light itself almost shines from this picture of Norham Castle, and it is hard to believe that Turner's public could not understand what he was painting. They were quite wrong when they thought that he was not looking closely at Nature, for sometimes he went to extremes just to study some effect of light.

In 1842 he painted a picture of a snowstorm at sea which is surely one of the most remarkable pictures of storms ever painted. You can feel the surge of the ocean waves and almost hear the shrill scream of the wind— yet people still said that it wasn't naturalistic! Such a picture could only have been done after a close study of the sea in storm. Turner had, in fact, gone on board a ship to watch the sea in bad weather, when a very fierce storm arose. Far from being frightened, Turner was fascinated by what he saw, but as he remained on deck there was a danger of his being swept overboard. He therefore ordered the sailors to lash him to the mast so that he could watch it in safety. He stayed there in the terrible gale, according to his own account, for over four hours. Surely such a magnificent picture was worth all that effort.

Another story told about Turner gives some idea of how he 'filled his mind with materials drawn from a close study of nature'. A young woman who was travelling in a train in 1844 was astonished to see the man opposite her suddenly take off his top hat and lean out of the window. He remained out for some minutes, in spite of the fact that it was raining very hard and the train was going at full speed. The man was Turner, and the result of this close study of nature is called 'Rain, Steam and Speed'.

Turner's understanding and ability to paint light was far ahead of his time—he was in fact called 'the father of the Impressionists' by one critic, though he died in 1851, long before Impressionism was thought of. So far ahead of his time was he that he was scarcely understood by his friends, and towards the end of his life he refused to exhibit or show his great paintings, for fear that people would think he was mad.

Turner. Snowstorm at sea. National Gallery, London

Turner. Rain, steam and speed—The Great Western Railway. National Gallery, London

Constable. Spring Ploughing. Victoria & Albert Museum, London

Palmer. Valley with a bright cloud. Ashmolean Museum, Oxford

nature and art

Not many artists have gone to quite the lengths that Turner did to study Nature, but most great artists have looked towards Nature as a guide and inspiration. Sometimes they have tried to show how beautiful Nature can be by copying its appearance as closely as possible. At other times they have distorted its appearance to pass on some special feeling they have about Nature itself.

Constable's picture of Spring ploughing is a very realistic picture. The artist has tried to paint the ploughed field as it really appeared with a slight breeze blowing over it. But his aim was more to capture the mood of the landscape than to record every detail of leaf and twig. To catch this mood he has used only a few colours, and a restful composition of horizontal lines. The framework of the picture is well balanced, with the windmill and horse team on the right balanced by the trees on the left. It is a soothing and refreshing landscape which departs very little from the sort of thing we can actually see for ourselves. Nature and her moods, to Constable's eyes, are sufficiently beautiful to be painted quite realistically. But realism which depends on detailed copying was never his aim, for he himself spoke about 'the absurdity of imitation'. He seeks to reveal Nature's moods, rather than to imitate her appearance.

Samuel Palmer drew this 'Valley with a Bright Cloud' not so much to reveal nature to our eyes as to comment on it. Unlike Constable, he didn't feel it sufficient to say, 'Look, this is Nature as I see her'. He preferred to say, 'Look, this is Nature as I feel her'. In his picture the trees are not realistically drawn at all. They remind us of the mediaeval drawings of a tree on page 54, where simple shapes are used to suggest the idea of a tree. All the natural forms in this picture, the trees, bushes, rocks and grasses, even the land itself, have a rhythm not found in the Constable.

Palmer was fascinated by the mystery of Nature: he believed that trees, streams and stones were alive and could talk in a language of their own. He said that he sometimes saw trees as living men. To express this hidden life, he distorted the natural appearance of things to add a richness of feeling which an exact copy could never do.

Graham Sutherland, a modern English painter, has taken this distortion of natural appearance very much further. Even his colour is unnatural. Both the sky and the ground are painted in reds, adding a strange feeling of dramatic life to the picture of the mountain.

Sutherland, like Palmer, was fascinated by the strange hidden life of nature, and felt that only by a definite kind of distortion could he convey what he felt. Perhaps his own words will make clear his attitude to Nature: 'In painting, by a deliberate method, one can underline the sensations of one's subject and shed a light on the nature of things and emotions.' His deliberate method is distortion, which he uses to underline his sensation of Nature in a very powerful way. If you look closely at this picture, you will begin to feel the strange atmosphere which he was wanting to convey.

Sutherland. Red landscape, 1942. Art Gallery, Southampton

Sutherland. Rearing tree form. Collection of
Sir Colin and Lady Anderton

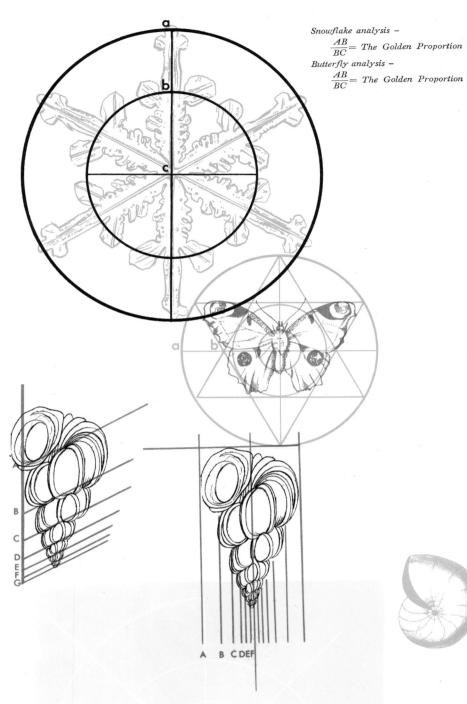

Snowflake analysis –

$$\frac{AB}{BC} = \text{The Golden Proportion}$$

Butterfly analysis –

$$\frac{AB}{BC} = \text{The Golden Proportion}$$

Bewick. Wood engravings. Author's collection.

Shell analysis –

$$\frac{BC}{AB} : \frac{AB}{AC} : \frac{CD}{BC} : \frac{BC}{BD} \ \ etc, etc.$$

Spiral (Phidias spiral)

$$\frac{BC}{AB} : \frac{AB}{AC} : \frac{CD}{BC} : \frac{BC}{BD} \ \ etc, etc.$$

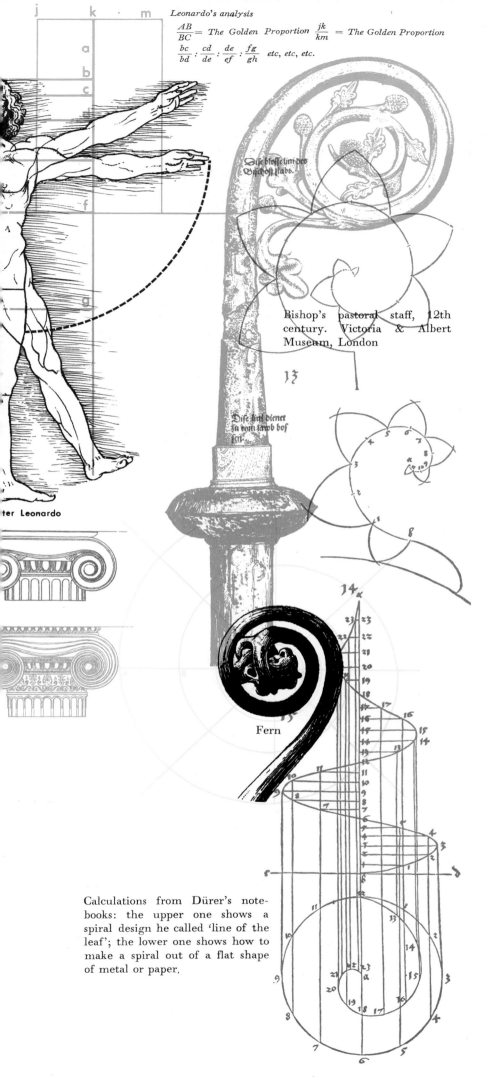

$\dfrac{AB}{BC}$ = The Golden Proportion $\dfrac{jk}{km}$ = The Golden Proportion

$\dfrac{bc}{bd} : \dfrac{cd}{de} : \dfrac{de}{ef} : \dfrac{fg}{gh}$ etc, etc, etc.

ter Leonardo

Bishop's pastoral staff, 12th century. Victoria & Albert Museum, London

Fern

Calculations from Dürer's notebooks: the upper one shows a spiral design he called 'line of the leaf'; the lower one shows how to make a spiral out of a flat shape of metal or paper.

snowflakes, spirals and curves

Sometimes, instead of being interested in a whole landscape or view, an artist takes an interest in one little piece of nature, like a single tree, a bird's nest or a feather. He often makes studies of such things so that he can put them into a larger picture.

Occasionally, however, an artist becomes interested in one thing for itself, and makes this the subject of his painting. How close Sutherland's view of Nature is to that of Palmer can be seen from this drawing of an old tree trunk, which is half monster rearing out of the ground in a most fearful way. Sutherland not only saw trees as living men, but actually drew them in that way.

It was said earlier that the golden proportion could be found in many natural forms, from the human body to a snowflake. Certain shells, as can be seen from the diagrams, are shaped on the golden proportion—as are the horns of some animals, and the shapes of flowers, ferns, butterflies and water currents. This has fascinated artists for centuries. Leonardo da Vinci did many drawings of natural forms showing their mathematical proportions, and Dürer's notebooks contain many little diagrams showing how interesting lines can be found in Nature.

An artist may sometimes study a natural object very closely in order to see how its mathematical proportions are arranged, and then use these proportions to create a work of art. One way of proving that a shell is built on the golden proportion is by tracing the shape of its spiral growth. Join the end of a pencil to the tip of a shell with a piece of cotton thread, and move the pencil around the shell so that the thread runs in the grooves. If the cotton is kept tightly in the grooves, you should draw a spiral.

It is not difficult to show that this spiral is based on the golden proportion—as can be seen from the diagram. The spiral is mathematical and at the same time can be found in nature. The Greeks knew of this spiral and used it in the design of their buildings and ornaments, as the top of the column (called a volute) shows. The Bishop's staff of 900 A.D. also appears to be based on the same kind of spiral.

Georges de la Tour. Madonna and Child. Musée de Rennes

colour

If you were to try to imagine a world where the trees, sky and flowers were all different shades of grey—you would quickly see how important colour is. 'All men enjoy colour,' said Ruskin, the art critic, 'it is meant for the delight of the human heart.'

Colour attracts us and interests us. It affects our feelings. When the sky is overcast with grey clouds, just before it begins to rain, all the world around is also grey, and we feel depressed and miserable. But when the sky is blue and sunshine is flooding the world with light, the colours around are bright, and we feel cheerful.

In art, as in nature, colours have a similar effect. See how the coloured reproduction is much more exciting to look at than the black and white one—even though they are both of the same picture.

Certain colours have a definite effect on our feelings. Red, for instance, is said to be a 'warm' colour, and is more exciting to the eye than, say, blue or green. We probably link up red with the idea of fire, and think of it as being warm.

Blue, on the other hand, is definitely a 'cold' colour— we even have a saying 'blue with cold'! When an artist wants to paint a picture full of life and gaiety, he will use warm colours, like reds and browns. When he wants to paint a picture full of sadness, or one of quiet

Tintoretto. Christ at the Sea of Galilee.
National Gallery of Art, Washington, D.C.

rest, he will use the 'cooler' colours, like blue and bluish greens.

The very definite effect that certain colours can have may be clearly seen from a comparison between the red picture by Georges de la Tour, which is how he painted it, and the picture in green. The 'feeling' of each picture is very different, yet only the colour has changed. The red is certainly more exciting than the green.

Some colours suggest certain impressions of distance. Blue is said to recede, or 'go back', while red is said to come forward. Artists often make use of this fact when they want to create a feeling of depth in their pictures.

The painting by Tintoretto is composed mainly of greens and blues, which give a strong sense of depth and at the same time suggest the stormy atmosphere. The red colour of Christ's robe in the foreground is put there especially to bring Him forward, and create a sense of distance between Him and the stormy waves behind.

Just as artists use a motif to link up the different parts of a pattern in a design, so they often choose a colour theme, which acts as a sort of motif, to link up the colours. In the picture by Holbein of Christina of Denmark, the colour theme is dark blue and grey. These are drab, slightly sad colours, which lend to the picture an air of quiet dignity—aided by the vertical lines of the composition. The small area of green floor and the fur add a little variety to the otherwise dull colour scheme. The white and pink of the face and hands form two areas which immediately draw our attention.

In this picture by Breughel the colour scheme is very gay and lively. Browns, yellows, reds, greens and white are all linked together in an exciting colour scheme which is suitable for a picture of peasants dancing. In both these paintings the colour theme is skilfully chosen to set a mood suitable to the subject painted: drab colours for the serious young princess, and gay, bright colours for the peasant dance.

Look back at a few pictures in this book and try to find ones where the colour sets the 'atmosphere' for the subject.

Breughel. The wedding dance. Detroit Institute of Fine Arts

Holbein. Christina of Denmark, Duchess of Milan. National Gallery, London

67

white dogs and blue horses

An artist can use colours in many different ways, depending on what effect he is wanting to give. This painting of a white dog and its puppy by Gainsborough is an example of the naturalistic use of colour. The artist's aim was quite simply to record the appearance of the dog and its puppy for the owner. This was in the days when photography was unknown, and the only way of recording the appearance of things was by drawing or painting. For this reason Gainsborough makes the dogs as realistic as possible. They are white dogs, so he would have been foolish to paint them red or orange.

The mediaeval artist who painted the blue horse to decorate his psalter wasn't interested in making the horse look realistic. He wanted to make a gay picture to entertain the eye, so he chose the brightest possible colours he could find. Blue horses certainly do not live in this world, but what a very exciting picture they make! This is the abstract use of colour, where the colours applied bear no resemblance to those which exist in actual life.

Colour can be used in a symbolical way—where it is taken to 'stand for' something. Young children usually paint in this way. They will use blue for the sky, even though the sky is not always blue; they will always use green for trees and plants and grasses—nearly always the same kind of green. Yellow will stand for the sun, and brown or black for the earth, even though these are not the natural colours of these things. In this way colours express ideas.

Gainsborough. White Pomeranian bitch. Tate Gallery, London

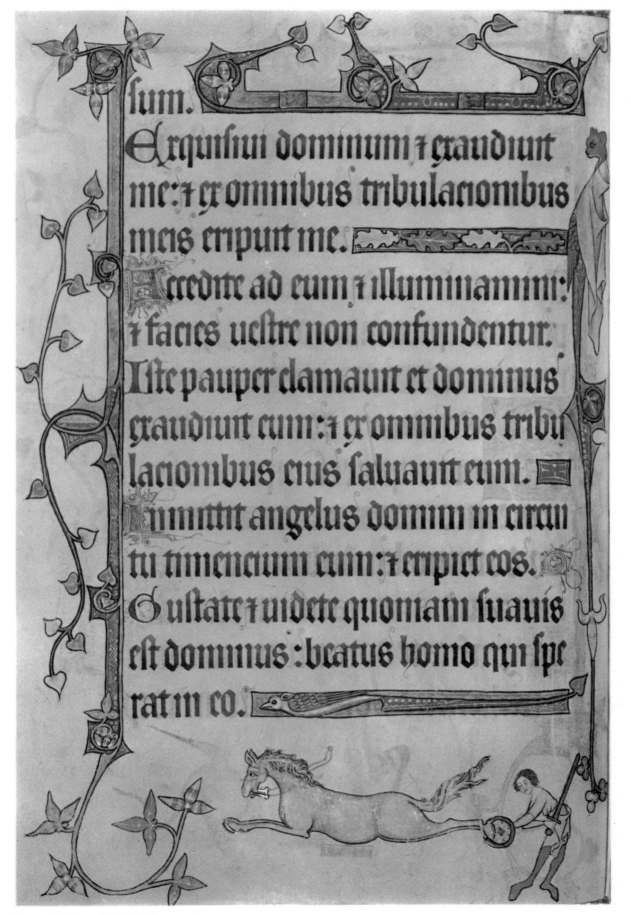

sum.

Exquisiui dominum z exaudiuit
me: z ex omnibus tribulacionibus
meis eripuit me.

Accedite ad eum z illuminamini:
z facies uestre non confundentur.
Iste pauper clamauit et dominus
exaudiuit eum: z ex omnibus tribu
lacionibus eius saluauit eum.
Immittit angelus domini in circui
tu timencium eum: z eripiet eos.
Gustate z uidete quoniam suauis
est dominus: beatus homo qui spe
rat in eo.

Luttrel Psalter. British Museum

expressionist colour

The Ancient Greeks used to paint most of their statues
with bright colours, in order to give an added feeling to
them. Over the hundreds of years since these statues
were made they have lost their colours, and we are left
with the white marble or brown wood from which the
statues were carved. Even in this state they look beautiful, but they must have lost a great deal of their
original appeal. Many primitive tribes use colour on
their carvings and masks, in an attempt to give a stronger
feeling than the uncoloured surface would. But in
most countries nowadays, sculptors tend to leave their
carvings and statues uncoloured, in the belief that the
subtle and delicate surface of marble, stone, wood or
metal is sufficiently interesting in itself.

You will remember that the Expressionist artist
distorts the natural appearance of things to pass on a
strong feeling. For the same reason an artist may use
very strong colours.

Stained-glass windows are often made more forceful
by the use of strong and expressionist colour. This head
of a saint would not have the same strength of feeling
if the colours were weaker or more naturalistic. In any
case it would have been rather silly of the designer to
give naturalistic colours to a distorted figure!

Edvard Munch, the Norwegian painter, makes quite
clear how colour alone can be used to pass on definite
and strong feelings. In the painting called 'The Cry'
Munch was trying to paint a picture of someone screaming. Like Picasso, he wasn't content with just drawing
a realistic picture of someone screaming—he had to
pass on a *feeling* of someone screaming. In some strange
way the colour and design achieve this. You can almost
feel the scream of the figure which is running like a
madman down the pier.

Stained glass, 12th century

Modigliani. Limestone head.
Chester Dale Collection, New York

Munch. The cry.
Oslo Municipal Art Gallery

'The Cry' was painted in 1893, but many years later
Munch wrote a short story which is almost a description
of the picture: 'He ran along the sea. The sky and water
took on the colour of blood. He heard cries in the air and
covered his ears. Earth, sky and sea trembled, and he
felt a great fear.'

We too, on looking at this picture, can almost feel this
great fear. 'The Cry' is expressionist painting at its best.

modern art

Just as artists of other periods painted pictures for a definite reason, so does the modern artist. But his purpose is sometimes very different today from what it used to be, and this must be remembered when looking at modern art. The modern artist aims at different things, and for this reason his pictures must be looked at in a different way. Very often people find modern art difficult to understand. They make the mistake of looking at modern painting in the same way as they look at any other kind of painting. This is the wrong thing to do, because the modern artist is not necessarily painting with the same purpose in mind. It is silly to judge a modern painter in the same way as you would judge a painter of the eighteenth or nineteenth century.

These two pictures of dogs will make this quite clear. The dog in 'Landscape with man holding a horse' by George Stubbs is a very fine realistic painting, done to record the appearance of the dog for its proud owner.

The painting by Balla, a modern Italian, on the other hand, is quite different. Many people who can easily appreciate the reality of Stubbs's dog will say that Balla's picture does not look very much like a dog, and is therefore a bad picture! But Balla didn't intend his picture to look like a dog—he was more concerned with painting movement, and he wanted to represent the dog walking, the moving feet of the lady, and the swinging chain. He does this by painting the feet and chain in different positions, as if he had taken several photographs at different times on the same film. The effect is of a jerking movement which reminds us of an old 'movie', where all the actors jerk about instead of moving in a smooth and natural way as they do in modern films.

It would be foolish for us to judge this painting in the same way as we judge Stubbs's painting. They were made for different reasons.

Similarly it would be silly to judge abstract art in the same way as you would judge any other form of art. One kind of abstract art is a form of painting and sculpting in which no attempt is made to represent anything. The painting by Manessier, a French painter, appears to have no subject—it is quite simply a pleasing arrangement of colours and shapes without any particular meaning.

Of course, abstract designs have been made before. Many Celtic artists decorated their Bibles with abstract geometric shapes; pottery was often decorated with such designs, and cloth was made with abstract pattern shapes almost at the beginning of history. In such things as these, though, the abstract shapes were used only to

Stubbs. Landscape with man holding a horse. Tate Gallery, London

Detail of dog from Stubbs's landscape

Balla. Dog on leash. Museum of Modern Art, New York

Manessier. Minus 12°. Tate Gallery, London

decorate objects serving some useful purpose. Never before have artists painted abstract pictures which serve no purpose other than to be looked at and enjoyed for their own sake.

Why should there be so much of a change in recent art that such abstract painting should so suddenly come into existence? The answer is not very simple, for there are many reasons for abstract art being practised as it is today.

The most important thing is to realise that abstract art had its beginnings in painting which aimed at representing the familiar world of our own experience. Over 60 years ago Monet, whose work we have already looked at, wrote: 'When you go out to paint, try to forget what objects you have before you, a tree, a house, a field or whatever. Merely think, here is a little square of blue, here is an oblong of pink, here a streak of yellow, and paint it as it looks to you.' Monet, as we know, was probing into the nature of the world as he could see it—the world of light and appearance. But from what he says, we can see that it is not a far step for an artist to start putting little patches of colour on the canvas without any reference to nature.

Another reason why painters became interested in abstract painting was because they were tired of the styles of their day, when naturalism and the mere copying of appearance was so popular. Photography was by then quite common, and there was no longer any need or demand for an artist to make exact records of appearance as before.

Artists and their patrons became bored with painting and sculpting in the same old way.

Van Gogh was one of the first to express this boredom, both in his approach to art and in what he said. He wrote to his brother one day, 'I believe in the necessity for a new art of colour, of design, and of the artistic life'. He once referred to one of his paintings of a chair as an abstract 'symphony in yellow and blue'—he obviously believed, like Mondrian after him, that painting could be a form of music to our eyes.

Van Gogh died over 70 years ago, yet he saw as early as then this need for a new art form. Such a new form of art was abstract painting. And one of his friends and fellow countrymen, Paul Cézanne, was the painter to start off the inquiry which eventually discovered this new way of expression.

Cézanne. Aix: rocky landscape. Tate Gallery, London
© S.P.A.D.E.M. PARIS 1962

cézanne and apples

Over a hundred years ago Cézanne set out to paint the world around him, not as he saw it, but as he knew it to be. For hours he would sit in front of simple objects, like a jug or a few apples, and examine them closely. Only after he had looked at them for a very long time would he start to paint, slowly and laboriously. His aim was to paint reality.

Now, as we said earlier, reality is a very complex thing. Even an apparently simple object like an apple is made up of an incredible number of qualities. An apple is of a certain colour, which changes as the light changes (as Monet knew so well!). It has also a thin skin which has a certain surface texture and feel about it—smooth or rough. An apple, too, is solid; it occupies a certain amount of space, and has a certain weight. It also has a distinctive shape—no apple is exactly like another, and each is individual. Some apples are fresh, others are old and tasteless. Some apples are soft, others hard. Apples have all these different qualities and many more besides. No artist could paint all these in one single picture.

Some of these qualities we can see with our own eyes —others we cannot see but *know* to be there. We can, for instance, see an apple's colour, but not its weight.

It was precisely these hidden qualities, like weight and solidity, that Cézanne was trying to paint. He was trying to pierce through the mere appearance of a thing to reach its inner and invisible reality. In this respect he was one of the first artists of the modern school. The best modern artists seek to go more deeply than mere appearance, and to paint the deeper, more hidden qualities in the world.

The word ABSTRACT comes from two Latin words *abs* and *traho*, which mean 'from' and 'draw'. The word originally meant 'draw from' or 'separate'. And this is exactly what good abstract painters try to do: they separate one or two of the hidden qualities from the world around them, and try to express them in paint. Some might try to paint things like memory or a religious feeling, whilst others might try to paint fear. Each artist is seeking to paint something different.

Cézanne. Still life with water jug. Tate Gallery, London

In his painting of a dog, Balla 'separated' the movement of the dog and tried to paint this. Although the finished painting does not look very naturalistic, Balla is still painting what exists in reality. This sort of painting does not ignore reality, as it would appear at first, but tries to go more deeply into it than has ever been done before.

Cézanne's new probing into the nature of reality was one of the things which started off the painters of today towards abstract art. The other thing, even stronger than Cézanne in its effect on art, was the development of science.

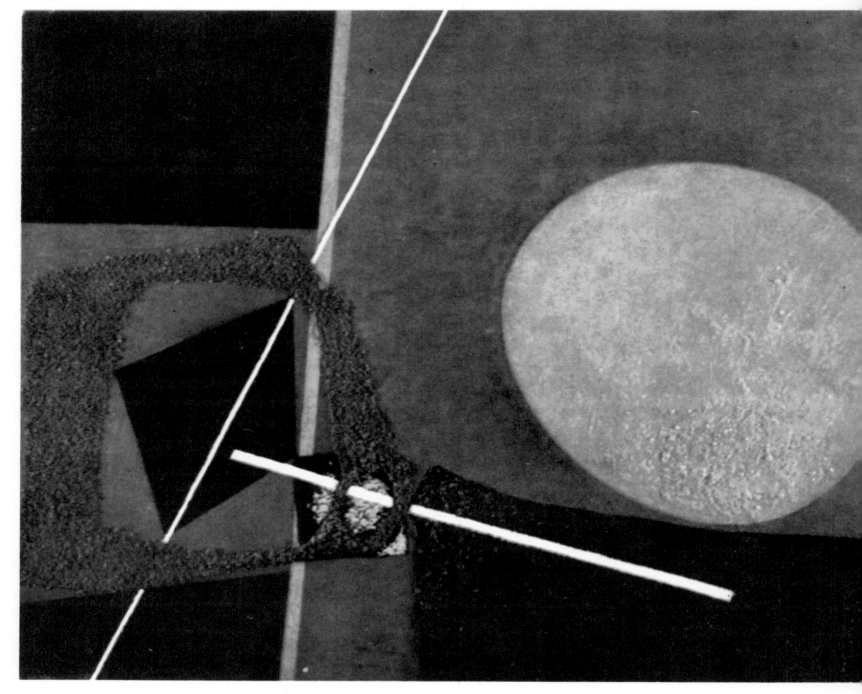

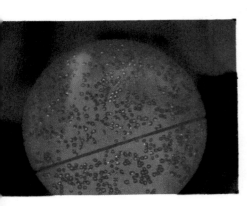

Microslide made by C. Wakstein
at Queen Mary College,
London University,
in author's possession

science and art

In the past few years, science has made tremendous progress. Man has been living in a civilised state for over six thousand years, and yet more advance in the way of inventions and scientific knowledge has been made in the last hundred years than in all previous time. If you imagine a twelve-inch ruler as representing the whole of Man's time on earth as a civilised being, less than a quarter of an inch on that ruler is the time in which all modern inventions have been made. Such a vast change in life — brought about by telephones, radios, television and aeroplanes in so short a time — has had a very great influence on the arts.

During this century scientists have made microscopes which can see clearly living things, hundreds of times thinner than a hair. Through these microscopes we see tiny creatures which live in worlds very different from our own. Many artists have become interested in these incredible worlds which, after all, are still part of Nature. They have used them as the basis for their paintings.

Besides looking down at Nature, through microscopes, scientists have also been looking up at the stars and out at space, through immense telescopes which probe into distances of millions of millions of miles. The almost unbelievable things seen in space, suns thousands of times greater than our own Sun, which is itself several thousand times greater than our Earth, have also fascinated artists. This picture by Prampolini, a modern Italian artist, could be of an immense blue sun, seen from some strange new planet, or it could equally be of a world seen under the microscope! Prampolini is exploring the unknown of painting, just as scientists are exploring the unknown of the universe. Both artists and scientists are experimenters.

Science today is showing us a strange new world. It teaches that the familiar world of solid shapes and light,

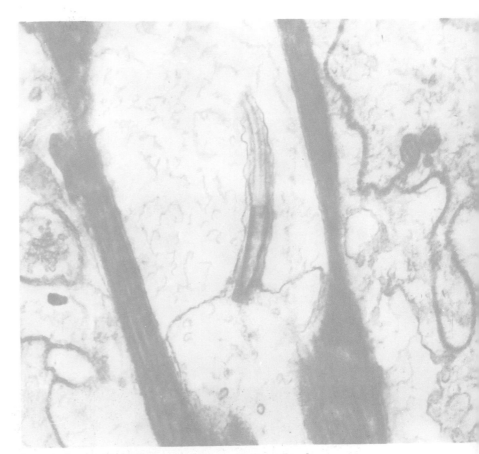

Microslide made by Dr Gray, University College, London.
By kind permission of the Royal Society

sound and colour, is in reality built up of electrical vibrations and waves, of tiny atoms and molecules. Our understanding of the world is changing very rapidly, and so, therefore, does our understanding of what reality is. With such astounding ideas as science presents, it is hardly surprising that one painter should exclaim, 'It's going to be more and more difficult for artists to paint only what they see with their eyes.'

What we see with our eyes is appearance, but what we know to be in the world of reality is day by day getting more and more amazing. This world of reality, so modern science teaches, is very different from the world as it appears to our eyes. Yet artists are trying, as never before, to express this hidden reality. Mondrian himself wrote: 'It is the task of art to express a clear vision of reality.' If science shows us that reality is very different from what we first assume, it is hardly surprising that our arts should change as much as our knowledge is changing.

Science is showing us a world of abstract forces and vibrations, and art is showing us a world of abstract colours and shapes. It is as if both art and science are joining hands to say: 'This world, as we see it, is only a thin cover for a deeper reality of abstract forms.'

three modern paintings discussed

Through the Rainbow. 1941. Joan Miro.

Not all modern artists are as interested in science as Prampolini. Some paint pictures of abstract shapes and lovely colours intended very simply to entertain the eye. There is no intention of these pictures 'looking like something'. They are, as one modern French painter says, 'just coloured paintings to which everyone can attach their dreams'.

The wonderful stained glass found in mediaeval churches was originally placed there so that worshippers could look at it to compose their minds before prayer. Some modern paintings can be looked at in the same way, as a rest for the eyes and a delight for the feelings. Another reason for having stained glass in windows was because the light coming into the church would be softened and changed into colour. This gave a religious atmosphere to the inside of the church and helped people to realise that they were on holy ground, in a world quite different from the one outside the church.

Paintings like 'Through the Rainbow' also seem to suggest another world, where quite different creatures could live. It is a delightful world of poetry, where the shapes, lines and colours suggest to the imagination many little shapes of animals, birds and fishes. It is the sort of picture which you can look at many times, and yet, on each occasion, find something different in it. 'The important thing,' said Miro, 'is the poetry in the painting.'

Stained glass from Chartres Cathedral, 13th century

Miro. **Through** the rainbow. Pierre Matisse Collection

Abstract Painting. 1955. Jackson Pollock

Some modern artists, like Jackson Pollock, use paint in a very curious manner. They let it dribble or splash in streaks all over their canvases. They even sometimes throw pots of paint at their canvases, and one artist has been known to ride a bicycle with painted wheels over his picture. Their aim is to make an interesting surface of paint, and an accidental colour arrangement which can often be pleasing to look at.

Artists call this 'action painting', whilst some people call it 'noodle soup' because the streaks of paint remind them of the long lengths of noodles. Such people say that paintings like this are silly—they claim that children can make similar pictures, or that they look no better than old walls or rusty dustbin lids. If such people were to look closely at children's paintings or at dustbin lids or old walls, they might be surprised to find that these can often be pleasant to look at. 'Everything,' a Chinese philosopher claimed, 'has its beauty—but not everyone sees it.'

The beauty of such a picture depends on how the accidents of colour and texture interest the eye, and on the way it affects our imagination and feelings. Five hundred years ago, Leonardo da Vinci observed that texture and stains on walls were useful things for suggesting subjects for compositions. He obviously found such things interesting and suggestive—perhaps even beautiful on occasion.

It would be foolish to judge a picture like this from a reproduction because it depends for its effects on paint itself. Try to find one in your local gallery of art, and have a look at it to find out what you really think about such painting.

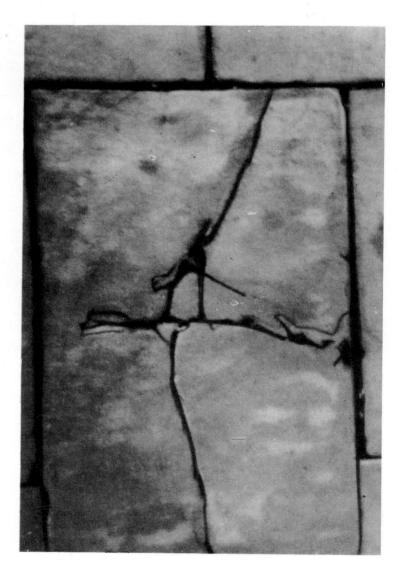

Photograph of cracked paving stone in author's collection

Pollock. Abstract painting, 1952. Tate Gallery, London

Metamorphosis of Narcissus. 1937. Salvador Dali

Dali is interested in painting dreams. We all know how the most peculiar things can happen in dreams, things which we know could not happen in the world around us. In Dali's paintings a giraffe can be on fire, or a set of drawers can be seen in someone's thigh. A watch can be turning into a piece of cheese, or a stone into a human being! Such things can happen in dreams.

This picture is called 'Metamorphosis of Narcissus'. Metamorphosis means 'a change in shape'. We can see how well Dali expresses this change, or metamorphosis, if we look at the picture, for everything seems to be changing. The immense hand holding the egg seems to be changing into a piece of stone, with ants crawling over it, whilst the chess board to the right is also a city square. The single chessman is turning into a statue in the middle of the square. Even the water of the stream appears to be changing into glass, for hardly a ripple disturbs the surface. We can see how clearly the rock-like hand echoes the shape of the human being in the stream, as if it is on the brink of changing into human shape itself.

The human being is Narcissus, who was a very beautiful Greek boy. He would not love anyone but himself, and as punishment for his selfishness the Greek gods made him fall in love with his own reflection in a stream. He would not leave his own reflection, even for food, and as a result he pined away with hunger. When he died he changed into a flower, which is still called after him.

It is as if this 'dream' painted by Dali really means: Narcissus, because he would love no one but himself, lost all he had, including himself, and was changed into a flower. His love was like an empty shell hatching out a single flower which cannot love at all.

Dali's painting, with its strange and eerie atmosphere, somehow conveys more of the meaning behind the story of Narcissus than the more realistic picture does.

J. W. Waterhouse. Echo and Narcissus. Walker Art Gallery, Liverpool

Dali. Metamorphosis of Narcissus. Tate Gallery, London

A knight from ivory
chess set, Isle of Lewis,
12th century.
British Museum

Flemish 14th century ewer.
Metropolitan Museum of
Art, New York, J. Pierpont
Morgan Collection

84

South German Christ
riding upon an ass,
16th century.
Victoria & Albert
Museum, London

Scandinavian bronze
ewer, 13th century.
Victoria & Albert
Museum, London

four horsemen

There is no exact definition of Beauty. When someone
says, 'That is a very beautiful work of art' what they
really mean is, 'To *me* that is a very beautiful work of
art'. Beauty—that is, the sense of beauty—is an emotion, and a very personal thing, private to each person.
Because of this, each person must find out for himself
what is beautiful and not rely on the judgment of others.
No man can say what is beautiful for another—he can
only say what is beautiful for himself.

Try an experiment to see how greatly people's tastes
can differ. Show this page of four horsemen to as many
of your friends as possible, and ask them which they
like most of all. You will very quickly find that there is
a wide difference in people's sense of beauty.

Statuette of Egyptian king,
13th Dynasty. British Museum

African mask of a Benin
king, 16th century.
British Museum

Modigliani. Gypsy woman with baby. National
Gallery of Art, Washington, D.C.

Bust of Charles II by Pelle.
Victoria & Albert Museum, London

86

King from ivory chess set,
Isle of Lewis, 12th century.
British Museum

Stained glass from Chartres Cathedral,
Madonna and Child

museums and art galleries

We all like different pictures and works of art, and we all have our favourite paintings; we might even have our favourite artists. Some of us prefer abstract styles of painting to pictures which tell a story. We all have different tastes, and this is how it should be. A rich variety of tastes is better than a boring similarity of likes and dislikes. Most art galleries and museums try to cater for this wide difference in tastes—though some do specialise, collecting and showing modern pictures or the older styles. After reading this book, it will be a good idea to take advantage of such museums and galleries, because by looking at pictures, you will learn much more than by merely reading about them.

What you learn from pictures depends very much on how you look at them. When you go to an exhibition you should not examine too many pictures in one visit. The mind and feelings become tired very easily. It is quite enough to look at seven or eight pictures at a time. If you give these few sufficient attention, you will learn more than if you spend an hour glancing at two hundred pictures.

Sometimes you can see people walking around an art gallery of ten or fifteen rooms, each with twenty or so paintings on show. These people will peer at every single picture on every single wall, as if it is their duty to do so! They might spend perhaps three or four seconds on each work of art. In other words, when they leave the gallery they will have seen every picture, but they will not have looked at a single one! Needless to say, they will not have enjoyed themselves. This is obviously a very silly way to regard art—better to choose one or two pictures and really enjoy them.

Try to look at pictures and other works of art as often as you can, because in this way an understanding of art will grow in your mind and feelings. And an understanding of art, which really means a love for art, can bring new meaning to your life, in the appreciation and enjoyment of its many beauties.

87

some important painters in the history of art

Name	Date	Country	Pronunciation
Angelico	c. 1387–1455	Italian	
Baldovinetti	c. 1426–1499	Italian	
Balla	1874–	Italian	
Bellini	c. 1430–1516	Italian	
Blake	1757–1827	English	
Bonnard	1867–1947	French	Bonnar
Bosch	c. 1450–1516	Netherlands	Bosh
Botticelli	c. 1445–1510	Italian	Bottichelly
Bouts	c. 1415–1475	Netherlands	Bowts
Braque	1882–	French	Brahk
Breughel	c. 1525–1569	Netherlands	Broyg-l
Canaletto	1697–1768	Italian	
Caravaggio	1573–1610	Italian	
Cézanne	1839–1906	French	Sezan
Chagall	1887–	French (born Russian)	Shagal
Chardin	1699–1779	French	Shardan
Claude	1600–1682	French	Clode
Constable	1776–1837	English	
Corot	1796–1875	French	Koroh
Correggio	c. 1489–1534	Italian	
Courbet	1819–1877	French	Koorbay
Crome	1768–1821	English	
Dali	1904–	Spanish	Dahly
Daumier	1808–1879	French	Dome-yay
David, Gerard	c. 1460–1523	Netherlands	
David, Jacques	1748–1825	French	Dahveed
Degas	1834–1917	French	D'ga
Delacroix	1798–1863	French	Delacrwah
Duccio	c. 1255–1319	Italian	Doochioh
Duchamp	1887–	French	Dooshon
Dufy	1877–1953	French	Doofy
Dürer	1471–1528	German	
van Dyck	1599–1641	Netherlands	van Dike
van Eyck	c. 1400–1441	Netherlands	van Ike
Fragonard	1732–1806	French	Fragonah
Francesca	c. 1415–1492	Italian	Franchesca
Gainsborough	1727–1788	English	
Gaugin	1848–1903	French	Gohgan
Giorgione	c. 1476–1510	Italian	Jorjoh-ny
Giotto	c. 1266–1337	Italian	Jottoh
van Gogh	1853–1890	French (born Dutch)	van Gof
Goya	1746–1828	Spanish	
el Greco	1541–1614	Spanish (born Greek)	
Grünewald	c. 1475–1528	German	Groo-ne-valt
Guardi	1712–1793	Italian	Gardy
Hobbema	1638–1709	Netherlands	
Hogarth	1697–1764	English	
Holbein	c. 1497–1543	German	Holbine
de Hooch	1629–1684	Netherlands	
Ingres	1780–1867	French	Angr

Klee	1879–1940	Swiss	Klay		Pollock		1912–1956	American	
de la Tour	1593–1652	French			Poussin	c 1593–1665	French	Poossan
Leonardo	1452–1519	Italian			Raphael		1483–1520	Italian	Rafile
Manet	1832–1883	French	Manay		Rembrandt		1606–1669	Netherlands	
Mantegna	c. 1431–1506	Italian	Mantaynya		Renoir		1841–1919	French	Renwahr
Martini	c. 1284–1344	Italian			Reynolds		1723–1792	English	
Masaccio	1401–1428	Italian	Masahcheeoh		Romney		1734–1802	English	
Matisse	1889–1954	French			Rouault		1871–1958	French	Roo-oh
Memlinc	c. 1430–1494	Netherlands			Rubens		1577–1640	Netherlands	
Michelangelo	1475–1564	Italian	Michael-anjelo		Ruisdael		1628–1682	Netherlands	Reesdale
					Seurat		1859–1891	French	Surah
Millais	1829–1896	English	Millay		Steen		1626–1679	Netherlands	
Millet	1814–1875	French	Millay		Stubbs		1724–1806	English	
Miro	1893–	Spanish	Meeroh		Sutherland		1903–	English	
Modigliani	1884–1920	French (born Italian)			Tintoretto		1518–1594	Italian	
Mondrian	1872–1944	French (born Dutch)	Mondri-ahn		Titian		1487–1576	Italian	Tishan
					Toulouse-Lautrec	1864–1901	French	Toolooz-Lohtrek
Monet	1840–1926	French	Monay						
Munch	1863–1944	Norwegian	Moonk		Turner		1775–1851	English	
Murillo	1617–1682	Italian			Uccello	c. 1397–1475	Italian	Oochello
Nicholson	1894–	English			Utrillo		1883–1955	French	
Palmer	1805–1881	English			Velasquez		1599–1660	Spanish	Vellaskez
Perugino	c. 1445–1523	Italian	Peroojino		Vermeer		1632–1675	Netherlands	
					Veronese	c. 1528–1588	Italian	
Picasso	1881–	Spanish			Watteau		1684–1721	French	Wot-oh
Pisanello	c. 1395–1455	Italian			Wilson	c. 1714–1782	English	
Pollaiuolo	c. 1432–1428	Italian	Pollai-oo-oloh		Zurbaran		1598–1664	Spanish	

INDEX